The Palermo Convention at Twenty

Transnational Crime

Volumes published in this Brill Research Perspective are listed at *brill.com/rptc*

The Palermo Convention at Twenty

The Challenge of Implementation

Edited by

Serena Forlati

BRILL

LEIDEN | BOSTON

This paperback book edition is simultaneously published as issue 3.4 (2019) of *Transnational Crime*, DOI:10.1163/24680931-12340019.

Library of Congress Control Number: 2021920492

Typeface for the Latin, Greek, and Cyrillic scripts: "Brill". See and download: brill.com/brill-typeface.

ISBN 978-90-04-46904-4 (paperback)
ISBN 978-90-04-46905-1 (e-book)

This book is printed on acid-free paper and produced in a sustainable manner.

Contents

Preface

This issue of *Brill Research Perspectives in Transnational Crime* focuses on the implementation of the United Nations Convention against Transnational Organized Crime and its Supplementing Protocols. It is part of a broader project, marking the UNTOC's 20th anniversary,[1] which started with *The Palermo Convention at Twenty – Institutional and Substantive Challenges* (Brill 2020) and aims at appraising the Convention's legal framework and its suitability as a tool for effectively combating present-day transnational organized crime. A third issue will conclude the series, addressing the relationship between the UNTOC and other branches of International Law.

The present issue discusses, firstly, the implementation of the parent Convention and each of the Supplementing Protocols. Andreas Schloenhardt, discusses the use of the UNTOC provisions on international cooperation – more specifically on extradition, mutual legal assistance, transfer of sentenced persons, transfer of criminal proceedings and joint investigations, while Fabrizio Sarrica assesses the achievements and the shortcomings in the implementation of the Human Trafficking Protocol and Simonetta Grassi addresses the Firearms Protocol. In these three settings, significant steps have been taken at the domestic level to ensure that domestic legislation is in line with the UNTOC and its Protocols; difficulties in implementing them rather lie in ensuring effective application of the relevant norms. Differently, in article 3, Alessandro Spena argues that an exclusively state-centered approach to migrant smuggling – as the one adopted at the EU level – hinders a correct implementation of the Smuggling of Migrants Protocol.

The second part of the issue focuses on the use of the Convention and its Supplementing Protocols in the fight against human trafficking and migrant smuggling, addressing selected issues that give rise to topical challenges and possible contradictions in the efforts to ensure effective implementation of the Convention system. These are, notably, the link between human trafficking and corruption (discussed by Rosana Garciandia), the protection of the victims of

1 This project is run in the framework of the Centre for European Legal Studies on Macro-Crime (Macrocrimes), of the Department of Law of the University of Ferrara, with the support of the Italian Ministry of University and Research (MUR-funded project 'Dipartimenti di eccellenza') and the Region Emilia-Romagna.

 | DOI:10.1163/9789004469051_002

trafficking and of victims more generally (addressed by Ruth Shrimpling and Annelies Blondé); the criminalization of NGOs conducting rescue operations at sea (dealt with by Laura Salvadego); finally, Eugenio Zaniboni reflects on the UNTOC provisions concerning undercover operations and their implementation in Italy.

This analysis cannot claim to offer a complete picture of the difficulties that the Contracting Parties and the international community more broadly face in ensuring an appropriate and effective implementation of the UNTOC. Nonetheless, it will hopefully encourage further discussion at a time when the launch of the UNTOC Review Mechanism[2] prompts the Contracting Parties to reconsider the adequacy of their domestic legal frameworks and operational capabilities in the fight against transnational organized crime.

Serena Forlati

2 See Conference of the Parties to the United Nations Convention against Transnational Organized Crime, Resolution 10/1, Launch of the review process of the Mechanism for the Review of the Implementation of the United Nations Convention against Transnational Organized Crime and the Protocols thereto.

International Cooperation under the United Nations Convention against Transnational Organized Crime

Expectations and Experiences

*Andreas Schloenhardt**

Abstract

This article examines the international cooperation provisions under the United Nations Convention against Transnational Organized Crime and their practical application in reported cases. It explores the circumstances in which States Parties have used or attempted to use the Convention as a legal basis for extradition, mutual legal assistance, transfer of sentenced persons, transfer of criminal proceedings, joint investigations, or other forms of international cooperation. The article seeks to provide a better understanding of the opportunities offered by the international cooperation provisions, and the challenges and obstacles faced by States Parties requesting cooperation or being requested to provide cooperation under the Convention.

Keywords

extradition – international judicial cooperation – mutual legal assistance – transfer of criminal proceedings – joint investigations

* Professor of Criminal Law, The University of Queensland; Honorary Professor of Foreign and International Criminal Law, University of Vienna. This article is based on research conducted by the author for the *Digest of Cases of International Cooperation in Criminal Matters involving the United Nations Convention against Transnational Organized Crime as Legal Basis* to be published by UNODC in 2021.

 | DOI:10.1163/9789004469051_003

Introduction

The need for comprehensive international criminal justice cooperation was one of the main motivators behind the development of the *United Nations Convention against Transnational Organized Crime* (UNTOC).[1] Such cooperation comprises a range of frameworks and practical measures that facilitate exchange and collaboration between States and their law enforcement, prosecution, and judicial authorities. The UNTOC creates avenues for obtaining evidence, accessing information, confiscating assets, transferring persons and proceedings, and arresting and returning fugitives across borders, thus "closing the gap that existed in international cooperation in an area generally regarded as one of the top priorities of the international community in the 21st century."[2] The provisions relating to international cooperation under the Convention include extradition (Article 16), mutual legal assistance (Article 18), joint investigations (Article 19), law enforcement cooperation (Article 27), transfer of sentenced persons (Article 17), transfer of criminal proceedings (Article 21), and the use of special investigative techniques (Article 20).

At this twentieth birthday of the UNTOC, it is timely to ask whether the Convention has achieved its stated purpose "to promote cooperation to prevent and combat transnational organized crime more effectively" (Article 1). This article examines the international cooperation provisions under the UNTOC and explores the circumstances in which States Parties have used the Convention as a legal basis. It gives insight into the opportunities offered by the Convention and the challenges and obstacles faced by States Parties.

1 Extradition

Article 16 of the UNTOC provides the legal basis and sets minimum standards for extradition for offences covered by the Convention.[3]

---

1 Opened for signature 15 November 2000, 2225 UNTS 209 (entered into force 29 December 2003); Alexandra Orlova and James Moore, "'Umbrellas' or 'Building Blocks': Defining International Terrorism and Transnational Organised Crime in International Law," *Houston Journal of International Law* 27 (2005): 285; also cited in Neil Boister, "The Cooperation Provisions if the UN Convention against Transnational Organised Crime: A 'Toolbox' Rarely Used?," *International Criminal Law Review* 19 (2016): 45.

2 Dimitri Vlassis, "The United Nations Convention against Transnational Organized Crime and its Protocols: A New Era in International Cooperation," in *The Changing Face of International Criminal Law* (Vancouver: ICCLR 2002), 75.

3 UNODC, *Criminal Justice Assessment Toolkit* (New York: United Nations, 2006), International Cooperation, 8.

1.1 *Scope and Application*

The obligation to extradite applies "to the offences covered by this Convention" (Article 16(1)). By reference to Article 3(1), this includes:

- offences established in accordance with Articles 5 (participation in an organized criminal group), 6 (money laundering), 8 (corruption), and 23 (obstruction of justice);
- serious crimes (defined in Article 2(b)); and
- offences established in accordance with the three Protocols supplementing the UNTOC.[4]

Article 3(1) requires that the offences to which the Convention applies must meet two criteria: they must involve an organized criminal group and must be transnational in nature. According to Article 3(2), an offence under the Convention is transnational in nature if it is committed

(a) in more than one State;
(b) in one State but a substantial part of its preparation, planning, direction or control takes place in another State;
(c) in one State but involves an organized criminal group that engages in criminal activities in more than one State; or
(d) in one State but has substantial effects in another State.

The obligation under Article 16(1) further applies "in cases where an offence referred to in Article 3(1)(a) or (b) involves an organized criminal group and the person who is the subject of the request for extradition is located in the territory of the requested State party". Under this alternative, transnationality of the offence is not strictly necessary.[5] Extradition under the first alternative of Article 16(1) further extends to "serious crime" as defined in Article 2(b), namely "conduct constituting an offence punishable by a maximum deprivation of liberty of at least four years or a more serious penalty".

---

4 Article 1(3) Protocol to Prevent, Suppress, and Punish Trafficking in Persons, especially Women and Children, opened for signature 15 November 2000, 2237 UNTS 319 (entered into force 25 December 2003), Article 1(3) Protocol against the Smuggling of Migrants by Land, Sea and Air, opened for signature 15 November 2000, 2241 UNTS 507 (entered into force 28 January 2004), and Article 1(3) Protocol against the Illicit Manufacturing of and Trafficking in Firearms, their Parts and Components, and Ammunition, opened for signature 31 May 2001, 2326 UNTS 208 (entered into force 3 July 2005).

5 UN Conference of the Parties to the United Nations Convention against Transnational Organized Crime, *Use of the United Nations Conventions against Transnational Organized Crime as a legal basis for international cooperation against all forms of transnational organized crime*, UN Doc CTOC/COP/WG.3/2015/3 (18 August 2015) 6 [29]; UNODC, *Manual on Mutual Legal Assistance and Extradition* (New York: United Nations, 2012), 26 [59], 46 [98].

The application of the Convention to offences punishable by four years imprisonment or more was relevant in a case reported by the Netherlands.[6] Dutch authorities spotted two persons who were sought by the Dominican Republic in relation to a murder committed by an organized criminal group. The Dominican Republic then filed an extradition request on the basis of article 16. This was initially complicated by the fact that Dutch extradition law did not allow extradition for a charge of murder. The law did, however, allow extradition for offences under the UNTOC. In April 2010, the extradition law was amended to allow extradition for any offence with a statutory penalty of four years or more when committed transnationally by an organized criminal group. The two suspects were arrested and extradited in May 2010.[7]

Article 16(1) further requires "that the offence for which extradition is sought is punishable under the domestic law of both the requesting State party and the requested State party". This dual criminality requirement reflects the *nullum crime sine lege* maxim.[8] Dual criminality made it possible for Romania to request extradition from Colombia. The accused in this case engaged in a tax fraud, document forgery, and money laundering scheme that resulted in a loss of EUR 870,000 to the Romanian State. Some of the transactions involved fraudulent sales of apartments in Colombia, where one of the accused, a Romanian national, was located. Using article 16 as the legal basis, Romania sought extradition of that person from Colombia, noting that money laundering had been made a criminal offence in both States pursuant to the UNTOC.[9]

1.2 *Relationship to Other Extradition Treaties*

The UNTOC can provide a basis for extradition in addition to other bilateral or multilateral agreements into which the States have entered. Article 16(3) obliges States Parties to treat the offences described in article 16(1) as automatically

6 UN Conference of the Parties to the United Nations Convention against Transnational Organized Crime, *Catalogue of examples of cases of extradition, mutual legal assistance and other forms of international legal cooperation on the basis of the United Nations Convention against Transnational Organized Crime*, UN Doc CTOC/COP/2010/CRP.5 (22 September 2010) 15–16 [80].

7 UN Doc CTOC/COP/2010/CRP.5, 15–16 [80].

8 Neil Boister, *An Introduction to Transnational Criminal Law* (Oxford; Oxford University Press, 2nd ed, 2018) 359; see further Robert Currie and Joseph Rikhof, *International and Transnational Criminal Law* (Toronto: Irwin Law, 2nd ed, 2014), 481.

9 UNODC SHERLOC Case Law Database, case identifier ROUx003, <https://sherloc.unodc.org/cld/case-law-doc/moneylaunderingcrimetype/rou/omn_and_mv.html?lng=en&tmpl=sherloc> (accessed 12 November 2020).

included in existing extradition treaties between them.[10] States Parties are further obliged to include them in all future extradition treaties between them.[11]

The effect of article 16(3) is reflected in an extradition case involving Croatia and the United States.[12] The accused set up a fictitious private equity firm in the US which defrauded developers by inducing them to make what they believed to be fully refundable deposits. He made representations that the deposits would be kept safe but, when asked, would then refuse to return the developers' money. Several other accused set up different entities and bank accounts in order to conceal the origin of the deposits and then used the money for their own benefit. In May 2012, one of the accused was arrested in Croatia and extradited. In proceedings before a District Court in Massachusetts in May 2014, he argued that his extradition was improper because the "rule of speciality" warrants that the offence he was tried for, conspiracy to commit money laundering, is deemed to be an extraditable offence by the requesting State and requested State and that the existing extradition agreement between the US and Croatia did not cover this offence. The Government instead argued that

> this "speciality" challenge must fail for three reasons: (1) Croatia clearly indicated its intent to extradite [the defendant] on the charge of conspiracy to commit money laundering, (2) US courts may try extradited defendants for crimes that involve similar conduct as that charged in an extradition order and (3) even if the crime of money laundering was not covered by the original extradition treaty and Croatia, the *United Nations Convention against Transnational Organized Crime* effectively amended the extradition treaty.[13]

The Court followed, by and large, the Government's position and further noted that both States are parties to the Convention which, inter alia, mandates that they classify money laundering as an extraditable offence.[14]

---

10 David McClean, *Transnational Organized Crime* (Oxford: Oxford University Press, 2007), 179.

11 UNODC, *Legislative Guide for the Implementation of the United Nations Convention against Transnational Organized Crime* (2nd ed, 2016) [494]–[495].

12 *US v Condo et al* (Criminal Action No 11-cr-30017-NMG, United States District Court, D Massachusetts, 7 March 2014, Gorton DJ).

13 *US v Condo et al* (Criminal Action No 11-cr-30017-NMG, United States District Court, D Massachusetts, 7 March 2014, Gorton DJ) [emphasis added].

14 *US v Condo et al* (Criminal Action No 11-cr-30017-NMG, United States District Court, D Massachusetts, 7 March 2014, Gorton DJ).

An extradition case request from the United States involves provisions under New Zealand's *Extradition Act 1999* that were introduced to reflect the obligations arising from article 16(3) and the second alternative paragraph (1). Between 2005 and 2012, the defendants were involved in copyright violations and money laundering schemes that caused losses in excess of USD 500 million to copyright holders. The defendants operated an online file-sharing system which, by January 2012, reportedly had 60 million registered users worldwide. In 2015, the US sought the extradition of four accused from New Zealand who were wanted for a range of charges relating to racketeering, copyright infringement, and wire fraud. In December 2015, the District Court in Auckland ruled that the men were eligible for extradition under the Treaty on Extradition between New Zealand and the United States of America[15] and New Zealand's *Extradition Act 1999*. The Court noted that US authorities had presented a "large body of evidence" to support a prima facie case. One of key issues in the accused's appeal to the High Court was the question of whether the offences set out in the indictment are extradition offences within the meaning of section 4 of the *Extradition Act*.[16] Section 11 of that Act states that section 4 may be overridden if an offence is an extradition offence listed in a treaty, such as the extradition treaty between the US and New Zealand. It is in this context that article 16 of the UNTOC became relevant. Following New Zealand's ratification of the Convention, section 101B was inserted into the *Extradition Act* which deems certain crimes with transnational aspects to be included in extradition treaties. This includes:

> any offence against any enactment if –
> (i) it is punishable by imprisonment for a term of 4 years or more; and
> (ii) the offence for which extradition is requested is alleged to involve an organized criminal group (as defined in article 2(a) of [the UNTOC]); and
> (iii) the person whose extradition is sought is, or is suspected of being, in or on his or her way to the requested country.

One of the main issues before the court concerned the question of whether the offence of "copyright infringement by digital online communication of copyright protected works to members of the public" is a criminal offence in New Zealand under the *Copyright Act*. While the District Court found this to be the case, the High Court disagreed.[17] The High Court did, however, find that the

15 Signed 12 January 1970, 22 UST 1 (entered into force 8 December 1970).
16 *Ortmann et al v The United States of America* [2017] NZHC 189.
17 Ibid.

offence of "conspiracy to commit copyright infringement" under US law corresponded to the New Zealand offence of "conspiracy to defraud" which is an extradition offence under the bilateral treaty. It further held that other charges against the accused corresponded to serious offences under New Zealand's *Crimes Act*. The High Court confirmed that the evidence presented satisfied a prima facie case against the appellants and ruled that they were eligible to be extradited.[18] In a further appeal, the New Zealand Court of Appeal overruled the High Court, arguing that extradition for the US copyright infringement offence is permissible as it is an equivalent offence in New Zealand to possess digital copyrighted works with an intention to disseminate them.[19]

In an extradition case involving the United States and Nigeria, the accused was charged in relation to fraudulent dealing in, and embezzlement of, distribution cheques. Together with other associates, the accused gained access to retirement accounts in the US by stealing the account owners' personal information which he then used to remove over USD 750,000 from their accounts. After one of the co-conspirators was caught in the US, the accused fled to Nigeria, where he was arrested. US authorities subsequently sought his extradition on the basis of the UNTOC and a bilateral extradition treaty.[20] In an extradition hearing before the Federal High Court in Lagos in January 2012[21] the accused argued that neither instrument had domestic application in Nigeria and that, as a result, the Court did not have jurisdiction to effect his extradition. The Government, in response, argued that the treaty had become domestic law through a legal notice and had been gazetted in 1967 and thus formed part of Nigeria's *Extradition Decree 1966*. The Court accepted this position and determined that the Decree was enforceable law and that the Court thus had jurisdiction. The Government further successfully argued that the offences identified in the extradition request were extraditable offences under Nigerian law as well as under the UNTOC.[22] The Court ultimately ordered that the accused be taken into custody pending his removal to the US, though it did not further comment on the Convention's domestic application in Nigeria and on the question of whether the offences were extraditable offences. The case nevertheless reflects the relationship between the UNTOC and existing

18 Ibid.

19 *Ortmann et al v United States of America* [2018] NZCA 233.

20 Signed 22 December 1931, 163 LNTS 59 (entered into force 24 June 1935).

21 *Attorney General of the Federation v Rasheed Abayomi Mustapha*, Charge No FHC/L/218C/2011 (Federal High Court Lagos, Judge P I Ajoku, 9 January 2012); see also, UNODC, *Cases and materials on extradition in Nigeria* (Abuja: United Nations, 2016), 510–542.

22 *Attorney General of the Federation v Rasheed Abayomi Mustapha*, Charge No FHC/L/218C/2011 (Federal High Court Lagos, Judge P I Ajoku, 9 January 2012).

extradition treaties and how Convention offences may be deemed to be part of such treaties, as envisaged by article 16(3).

1.2.1 Treaty- and Statute-Based Extradition

Article 16(4) allows, but does not require, States Parties to use the Convention as a treaty basis for extradition if such a treaty basis is a prerequisite.[23] In these circumstances, UNTOC may serve as a "surrogate extradition convention".[24]

For example, article 16(4) was used to enable the extradition of a suspected migrant smuggler from Italy in 2013. The accused was involved in a venture that departed from the Dominican Republic in March 2011, intending to bring three migrants to Miami, Florida. The vessel capsized and while the smugglers were able to swim to shore, the migrants drowned. One of the smugglers was arrested a few days after he returned to the Dominican Republic.[25] He was able to flee from custody, was arrested again, released from pre-trial detention on bail, and then absconded to Italy. Dominican authorities subsequently issued an INTERPOL Red Notice which led to his arrest in Italy in March 2013.[26] The Dominican Republic then submitted a request for his extradition. In the absence of any bilateral extradition treaty between the two countries, article 16(4) was cited as the legal basis. Italian authorities approved the request in May 2013 and the accused was subsequently returned to the Dominican Republic,[27] where he was sentenced to imprisonment for 15 years.[28]

---

23 UN Doc CTOC/COP/WG.3/2015/3, 6 [26].

24 Boister, *Introduction*, 358.

25 José A. Thomas, "Sometem yolero por desaparición de dos hombres," *El Nacion* (online), 12 March 2011 <https://elnacional.com.do/someten-yolero-por-desaparicion-de-dos-hombres/> (accessed 12 November 2020).

26 Adonis S. Díaz, "Interpol detiene promotor de viajes ilegales," *Diario Libre* (online), 28 March 2013 <https://www.diariolibre.com/actualidad/interpol-detiene-promotor-de-viajes-ilegales-FMDL377130> (accessed 12 November 2020).

27 Néstor Medrano, "Extraditan desde Italia a un domicano estaba prófugo," *Listin Diario Santo Domingo* (online), 18 June 2013 <https://listindiario.com/la-republica/2013/06/18/281118/extraditan-desde-italia-a-un-dominicano-estaba-profugo> (accessed 12 November 2020); [s.n.], "Condenan hombre por actuar en comlicidad con capitán de yola," *El Nacional* (online), 23 July 2013 <https://elnacional.com.do/condenan-hombre-por-actuar-en-complicidad-con-capitan-de-yola/> (accessed 12 November 2020); [s.n.], "Cinco años de cárcel para un hombre por complicidad con capitán de yola donde murieron tres personas," *Listin Dirario* (online), 24 July 2013 <https://listindiario.com/la-republica/2013/07/24/285547/cinco-anos-de-carcel-para-un-hombre-por-complicidad-con-capitan-de-yola-donde-murieron-tres-personas> (accessed 12 November 2020).

28 UNODC SHERLOC Case Law Database, case identifier, case identifier DOM006 <https://sherloc.unodc.org/cld/case-law-doc/migrantsmugglingcrimetype/dom/2016/sentencia_num._422_de_suprema_corte_de_justicia_segunda_sala.html?lng=en&tmpl=sherloc>.

The question of how the UNTOC can be used to extradite a fugitive in the absence of an extradition treaty between two States stands at the heart of a 2013 case before the Supreme Court of British Columbia. The accused allegedly assisted in the planning of a robbery of a post office vehicle that was carried out by an organized criminal group in Gdansk in October 1999. It was further alleged that he was involved in an earlier heist which led to his association with the group and the 1999 robbery. The accused was later apprehended in Canada. In December 2009, Poland sought his extradition on the basis of article 16 of UNTOC and the request was approved in July 2013 by the Supreme Court of British Columbia.[29] The accused then applied for a stay of proceedings under the *Canadian Charter of Rights and Freedoms*, arguing that Poland misused the Convention as a "backdoor" approach to effect his extradition for an offence under domestic Polish law for which no bilateral treaty with Canada existed. The Court did not find an abuse of process and dismissed this argument.[30] The accused was later extradited to Poland on charges relating to robbery and participation in the activities of, and committing indictable offences for, an organized criminal group.

The way in which the UNTOC can enable extradition between States that have no bilateral treaties and are not both parties to another extradition agreement is well demonstrated in a case involving the United Arab Emirates (UAE) and the Netherlands. The extradition request made by the UAE followed an armed robbery of a jewellery store in a Dubai shopping centre in April 2007. The suspect in this case was believed to be part of the notorious "Pink Panther" group which specialises in thefts and robberies from jewellery stores and is believed to have some 800 members and to be responsible for nearly 300 robberies in 35 countries since 1999.[31] When the UAE first requested extradition of this suspect, the Netherlands refused the request in the absence of any legal basis to grant extradition. In May 2007, the UAE ratified the UNTOC and resubmitted its extradition request to the Netherlands. The High Court in The Hague then granted the request on the basis of the Convention and the suspect was extradited in February 2009. Later investigations, however, revealed that this person was not involved in the heist.[32]

29 *Poland (Republic) v Grynia* [2013] BCSC 1203.

30 *Poland (Republic) v Grynia* [2013] BCSC 1277.

31 Havana Marking, "The Pink Panthers: hunting the world's best diamond thieves," *The Guardian* (online), 22 September 2013 <https://www.theguardian.com/uk-news/2013/sep/22/pink-panthers-diamond-thieves-documentary> (accessed 12 November 2020).

32 UN Doc CTOC/COP/2010/CRP.5, 15 [79]; UNODC, *Manual*, 28; N Barakat, "'Pink Panther' heist: Fourth suspect to go on trial, Dubai Police reveals," *Gulf News* (online),

1.2.2 Article 16(5)

Under article 16(5)(a), States Parties that require a treaty basis for extradition must notify the Secretary-General as to whether or not they will permit UNTOC to be used for extradition. As of 4 October 2016, 31 States Parties had filed formal notifications that they would take the Convention as the legal basis for extradition (some specifying additional conditions) and 14 States Parties declared that they would not do so or did not expressly declare whether or not they would.[33] The majority of States Parties have made no statement either way, "possibly because they may be able to do so on the basis of their legislation but do not want to commit themselves, or because they will insist on reciprocity".[34]

It will generally not be possible to effect extradition from another State Party that makes extradition conditional on an existing treaty and does not accept the UNTOC as a legal basis. This problem arose, for instance, when in 2006 and 2008 Lithuania sought extradition from Kuwait of one of its citizens who was wanted on charges relating to participating in an organized criminal group, violating public order, and involving a child in a criminal act. The extradition request was made solely on the basis of UNTOC and was rejected because Kuwait did not accept the Convention as a legal basis.[35]

A similar position was expressed by the Federal High Court of Nigeria in relation to a request made by the Netherlands for the extradition of an accused sought on charges relating to trafficking in persons, smuggling of migrants, document fraud, abduction of minors, and participating in an organized criminal group.[36] Acting as part of an organized criminal group, the accused allegedly recruited six women in Nigeria, provided them with accommodation, arranged for their transportation, furnished them with fraudulent documents, and instructed them to apply for asylum upon arrival in the Netherlands. Dutch authorities later uncovered the group and charged and convicted three of its members.[37] An arrest warrant for the accused was issued and

---

19 October 2015 <https://gulfnews.com/uae/crime/pink-panther-heist-fourth-suspect-to-go-on-trial-dubai-police-reveals-1.1603048> (accessed 12 November 2020).

33 UN Conference of the Parties to the United Nations Convention against Transnational Organized Crime, *Working Group on International Cooperation established by the Conference of the Parties to the United Nations Convention against Transnational Organized Crime: an overview of mandates and work since its establishment*, UN Doc CTOC/COP/WG.3/2016/CRP.1 (6 October 2016) 2 [4]–[6].

34 Boister, "Cooperation Provisions," 55.

35 UN Doc CTOC/COP/2010/CRP.5, 6 [22].

36 *Attorney-General of the Federation v Edegbe*, suit no FHC/ABJ/CS/907/2012 (1 July 2014, Federal Court, Abuja, Lord Justice A R Mohammed).

37 *Attorney-General of the Federation v Edegbe*, suit no FHC/ABJ/CS/907/2012 (1 July 2014, Federal Court, Abuja, Lord Justice A R Mohammed).

communicated to Nigeria along with an extradition request. This request was heard by the Federal High Court in July 2014.[38] The central question in the case was whether by signing the Convention on 13 December 2000, the UNTOC, "without more, should qualify as a treaty for the purpose of extradition?"[39] The Court answered this question in the negative. It pointed out that Nigeria had several extradition treaties with other countries and that these treaties had been given effect in domestic law through acts of parliament. The UNTOC had not been given domestic effect in this way: "until it is made enforceable by an Act of the National Assembly, [a treaty] cannot apply in any proceedings before the Courts in this country".[40] The Court concluded that it had no jurisdiction over the case and refused to consider the Government's request to surrender and extradite the accused.[41]

1.3 *Conditions and Execution of Extradition*

Differences between prosecutorial practices can make effective international cooperation difficult. In the field of extradition, such differences are even more acute in relation to the documents to be presented to the requested State and the evidentiary requirements for granting an extradition request.[42] Modern extradition practice tends to simplify requirements with respect to the form of extradition requests and the channels of transmission, as well as the evidentiary standards. Accordingly, article 16(8) encourages States Parties to expedite extradition procedures and simplify evidentiary requirements in respect of the offences set forth in article 16(1).[43]

The evidentiary threshold required to authorize extradition on the basis of the Convention was the subject of proceedings before Maltese courts

38 *Attorney-General of the Federation v Edegbe*, suit no FHC/ABJ/CS/907/2012 (1 July 2014, Federal Court, Abuja, Lord Justice A R Mohammed).

39 *Attorney-General of the Federation v Edegbe*, suit no FHC/ABJ/CS/907/2012 (1 July 2014, Federal Court, Abuja, Lord Justice A R Mohammed).

40 *Attorney-General of the Federation v Edegbe*, suit no FHC/ABJ/CS/907/2012 (1 July 2014, Federal Court, Abuja, Lord Justice A R Mohammed). citing *Abacha v Fawehinmi* (2005) 51 WRN 29; B. Ezeamalu, "Human Trafficking: Judge refuses to extradite alleged Nigerian trafficker to Netherlands," *Premium Times* (online), 2 July 2014 <https://www.premiumtimesng.com/news/164260-human-trafficking-judge-refuses-to-extradite-alleged-nigerian-trafficker-to-netherlands.html> (accessed 12 November 2020).

41 See also Ezeamalu, "Human Trafficking".

42 UNODC, *Manual*, 15 [39]; McClean, *Transnational Organized Crime*, 182; Currie and Rikhof, 484–485.

43 UNODC, *Legislative Guide*, [516].

following an extradition from Chile.[44] The case involved a fraudulent investment scheme that resulted in charges relating to financial fraud and money laundering. In 2011, the accused and his mother set up an investment and wealth management firm that offered interest payments to investors. By the time Chilean authorities charged the accused, the scheme was worth some USD 40 million. The accused then fled to Malta, where he was later arrested.[45] In April 2017, the Court of Committal considered Chile's extradition request. In the absence of other applicable treaties, the Court turned to the UNTOC as the sole possible legal basis. The Court denied the request because of a "lack of admissible evidence that satisfies this Court that the [extradition] criteria in terms of article 16 of the Palermo Convention have been fulfilled in relation to the offences for which the Chilean Authorities request the suspect and as proffered in the Minister's Authority to proceed". Referring to article 8 of Malta's *Extradition Act*, the Court concluded "that the prosecution failed to sufficiently prove that the offences with which the suspect is accused in Chile are extraditable offences in accordance with the Palermo Convention."[46] The Attorney-General appealed, arguing, in general terms, that the evidentiary requirements should be interpreted less restrictively and suggesting that the Court of Committal should merely determine "on a prima facie basis, whether the requested person has a case to answer and whether the offences are extraditable ones at law". The Court of Criminal Appeal rejected these arguments, stating that "[o]n a practical level this would mean that a Maltese Court is rendered irrelevant as it must accept all that the Attorney-General declares that is admissible and acceptable and stop at that. Quite frankly this would usher in an era where one does not need the courts anymore".[47] The Court thus upheld the essential function of the judiciary in extradition proceedings under Maltese law and, by extension, the separation of powers. But the case also highlights the difficulties faced by requesting States in seeking to fulfil

44 *Police (Inspector Scannura) v Rajii* (Court of Magistrates (Malta), Magistrate Dr AM Bugeja, 7 April 2017).

45 *Police (Inspector Scannura) v Rajii* (Court of Magistrates (Malta), Magistrate Dr AM Bugeja, 7 April 2017).

46 *Police (Inspector Scannura) v Rajii* (Court of Magistrates (Malta), Magistrate Dr AM Bugeja, 7 April 2017).

47 Quoted in Edwina Brincat, "Multimillionaire accused of ponzi scheme will not be extradited," *Times of Malta* (online), 6 November 2018 <https://timesofmalta.com/articles/view/chilean-multimillionaire-will-not-be-extradited.693600> (accessed 12 November 2020).

high evidentiary standards under the domestic law of the requested State in extradition cases.

1.4 *Refusal of Extradition*

Article 16(14) provides that nothing in the Convention is to be interpreted as imposing an obligation to extradite if the requested State has substantial grounds for believing that the request has been made for the purpose of prosecuting or punishing a person on account of that person's sex, race, religion, nationality, ethnic origin or political opinions, or that compliance with the request would cause prejudice to that person's position for any one of those reasons.[48]

An issue of this kind was raised in an application for judicial review submitted to the Ontario Court of Appeal by a person whose extradition was sought by Slovenia using the UNTOC as the legal basis. The applicant suggested that he might face a risk of persecution should he be extradited. In this context, he argued that section 44(1)(b) of the *Extradition Act 1999* (Canada) prohibits extradition to a place where the person faces a risk of persecution and that the balance of probabilities would suffice to prove that risk. The Court rejected this argument and found that the judicial system of Slovenia was sufficiently fair and would not give rise to any concerns about the potential for persecution. An application for leave to appeal this decision was rejected.[49]

2 Mutual Legal Assistance

Under article 18(1), States Parties are required to provide the widest measure of mutual legal assistance in relation to the offences covered by the Convention. Article 18(1) further requires the provision of mutual legal assistance where the requesting State has reasonable grounds to suspect that the offence is transnational in nature and that the offence involves an organized criminal group.[50] Article 18(6) and (7) address the interplay between the Convention and bilateral and multilateral mutual legal assistance treaties. The UNTOC does not override any existing treaty already in place between States Parties (art 18(6)). Instead, the Convention gives States the option to use article 18(9)–(29) if this would facilitate cooperation. Where no other agreement binds the

---

48 See further UNODC, *Manual*, 52–53 [115]–[119].

49 *Soba v Slovenia* [2011] SCCA 177.

50 UNODC, *Legislative Guide*, [547].

parties, article 18(7) encourages States to use these provisions as a framework for mutual legal assistance. For this reason, article 18 has been referred to as "a mini mutual legal assistance treaty" in its own right.[51]

Article 18(3) sets forth eight specific types of mutual legal assistance that States Parties must be able to provide. The list of purposes for which assistance may be sought under article 18(3) is not exhaustive; it extends to "any other type of assistance" so long as the assistance does not contravene the domestic law of the requested country (art 18(3)(i)).

2.1 *Taking Evidence or Statements from Persons*

In cases involving transnational organized crime, witnesses and victims of a crime, along with other persons who have relevant information, are frequently located abroad. This will make it necessary to ask the State where those persons are located to take evidence or statements (art 18(3)(a)).

For example, in a case involving the laundering of proceeds deriving from drug trafficking through foreign banks and offshore companies, Brazil sought mutual legal assistance from as many as 23 other States. Thirteen of these requests were made on the basis of in order to hear witnesses, obtain banking information relating to the defendants, and freeze bank accounts. Although some requests were still pending at the time this case was reported, Brazilian authorities stressed that the information thus obtained was vital in order to enable the commencement of criminal proceedings against the defendants and could not have been obtained through channels other than the UNTOC.[52]

In a mutual legal assistance request addressed to Brazil, Swiss prosecutors urgently sought the hearing of a witness residing in Brazil at that time. The Brazilian Central Authority specifically advised Swiss authorities to transmit the request on the basis of the Convention "in order to eliminate bureaucratic delays and speed up the process within Brazil".[53]

A statement sought from a high-profile accused on the basis of UNTOC is at the heart of a prominent case involving Equatorial Guinea and France. In 2008, the Vice-President of Equatorial Guinea, who is also the son of the country's President, was accused by French authorities of embezzling state

---

51 UNODC, *Manual*, 2 [4]; UN Doc CTOC/COP/WG.3/2015/3, 5 [25], 6 [27]; Boister, "Cooperation Provisions," 52.

52 UN Conference of the Parties to the United Nations Convention against Transnational Organized Crime, *Catalogue of examples of cases of extradition, mutual legal assistance and other forms of international legal cooperation on the basis of the United Nations Convention against Transnational Organized Crime*, UN Doc CTOC/COP/2008/CRP.2 (17 September 2008) 3 [9]–[12].

53 UN Doc CTOC/COP/2008/CRP.2, 5 [26]–[27].

funds while he was Minister of Forestry and Agriculture and taking the proceeds from a tax that he levied on wood sales to support his lavish lifestyle. Allegations of money laundering and corruption against the accused and his family had previously been investigated by the United States Senate, leading to a settlement of USD 30 million with the US Department of Justice.[54] Following a complaint lodged in 2008, a public prosecutor in Paris launched a criminal investigation of the accused. As part of this investigation, France sought mutual legal assistance from Equatorial Guinea. The request asked for the accused to be questioned in relation to offences of money laundering and stated that: "[i]n the absence of a treaty on mutual legal assistance in criminal matters between France and Equatorial Guinea, this request is made on the basis of the United Nations Convention against Transnational Organized Crime".[55] The accused declined to answer questions, arguing that he was immune from the jurisdiction of foreign courts. The investigation was completed in 2016 and resulted in the accused being charged with money laundering by French prosecutors. In 2017, the accused was convicted in absentia by a French court and sentenced to a suspended term of imprisonment of three years and a suspended fine of EUR 30 million. The court also ordered the seizure of the accused's assets in France, including a building in Paris.[56] In 2016, Equatorial Guinea brought a case against France in the International Court of Justice (ICJ), seeking a suspension of the criminal proceedings and preventing France from seizing the building in Paris on the basis of diplomatic inviolability. The building had been designated an embassy of Equatorial Guinea. In a decision dated 6 June 2018, which followed a preliminary hearing on jurisdiction, the ICJ held that it did not have jurisdiction under the UNTOC to determine Equatorial Guinea's claims that (1) the criminal proceedings initiated by France unlawfully interfered with Equatorial Guinea's internal affairs and that (2) the accused was entitled to immunity. The Court stated that the dispute did not concern France's implementation of its obligations under the

54 Anton Moiseienko, "Introductory Note to Immunities and Criminal Proceedings (Equatorial Guinea v. France): Request for the Indication of Provisional Measure (I.C.J.)," *International Legal Materials* 57 (2018): 201; Lucas Olo Fernandes, "Oil, Instagram and the Plunder of Equatorial Guinea," *New York Times* (online), 27 November 2017 <https://www.nytimes.com/2017/11/27/opinion/equatorial-guinea-obiang-vice-president-corruption.html> (accessed 12 November 2020).

55 Martins Paparinskis, "'Introductory Note to Immunities and Criminal Proceedings (Equatorial Guinea v. France): Preliminary Objections (I.C.J.)," *International Legal Materials* 2019: 1.

56 Immunities and Criminal Proceedings (Equatorial. Guinea v. France), Provisional Measures Order, 2016 ICJ Rep. 1148 (Dec. 7); Moiseienko, "Introductory Note," 201.

Convention.[57] The Court did, however, hold that it had jurisdiction to determine Equatorial Guinea's claim that the searches and seizure of the Paris building were in breach of the *Vienna Convention on Diplomatic Relations*.[58] The case was still in progress at the time of writing.

2.2 *Searches, Seizures, and Freezing*

Under article 18(3)(c), a State Party may request another to conduct searches, seize assets or freeze bank accounts. Article 12 provides additional guidance on the freezing and seizure of proceeds of crime and of property, equipment, and other instrumentalities used in or destined for offences covered by the UNTOC.

The search of premises and the seizure of business records were the subject of a mutual legal assistance request made by the United Kingdom to Monaco in a case involving allegations of bribery and other corrupt practices. The UK's Serious Fraud Office identified three suspects who were believed to be residing in Monaco. Monegasque authorities subsequently searched premises, seized documents, computers, and other properties, and also arrested three persons.[59] In its letter requesting assistance from Monaco, the Serious Fraud Office made express reference to the *European Convention on Mutual Assistance in Criminal Matters*[60] and the UNTOC as the legal bases. This letter was the subject of the proceedings before the High Court of Justice.[61] The claimants (several alleged offenders) sought the quashing of the letter of request, return of materials obtained by the authorities in Monaco, and destruction of any copies of those materials held by the Serious Fraud Office. The High Court was asked to decide whether or not the common law duty of disclosure of evidence applied to letters of request from foreign authorities. The Director of the Serious Fraud Office argued that the duty of disclosure, as it applied to domestic search warrants, did not apply to such letters. In its decision, the High Court followed this position, thus rejecting the claimants' application.[62]

The freezing of bank accounts was the subject of a mutual legal assistance request made by Senegal to Monaco on the basis of article 18 of UNTOC in an

57 Immunities and Criminal Proceedings (Equatorial. Guinea v. France), Preliminary Objections, 2018 ICJ No 163 (Jun 6).

58 Opened for signature on 18 April 1961, 500 UNTS 95 (entered into force 24 April 1964).

59 Kevin Rawlinson, "Authorities in Monaco raid oil firm HQ in corruption investigation," *The Guardian* (online), 1 April 2016 <https://www.theguardian.com/business/2016/apr/01/authorities-monaco-raid-oil-firm-unaoil-hq-corruption-investigation> (accessed 12 November 2020).

60 Opened for signature 20 April 1959, ETS No 30 (entered into force 12 June 1962).

61 *R (Unaenergy and others) v Director of the SFO* [2017] EWHC 600.

62 *R (Unaenergy and others) v Director of the SFO* [2017] EWHC 600, [38].

unjust enrichment case. In June 2014, the Court of Appeal of Monaco granted the Senegalese request. The Director of Judicial Services of Monaco then asked the Prosecutor-General to execute a further request received from Senegal's Cour de la repression de l'enrichissement illicite, resulting in the freezing of 24 bank accounts. Among the affected account holders were two companies headquartered in the British Virgin Islands that subsequently lodged a complaint against the freezing of their accounts. The complaint was rejected by the Director of Judicial Services, as was a further appeal submitted to the Supreme Court of Monaco.[63] In the appeal to the Supreme Court, the appellants claimed, inter alia, that the request submitted by Senegal insufficiently established the existence of an organized criminal group, did not sufficiently specify the illicit origin of the funds in question, and involved an excessive infringement of the property rights of third parties. In June 2015, the Supreme Court rejected the appeal and declared that it had no jurisdiction (as argued by the Director of Judicial Services). A further complaint filed by the companies was rejected by the Cour de revision on 3 March 2016.[64]

2.3 *Providing Information, Evidentiary Items, and Expert Evaluations*

Article 18(3)(e) broadly refers to requests to obtain information, evidentiary items, and expert evaluation from another State Party. The supply of evidence under article 18(3)(f) is only unproblematic if that evidence is in possession of the requested State. Otherwise the measure may either require permission from the owner or the person in possession of that item or may require seizure of the item (art 18(3)(c)).[65]

A request for information about persons, financial transactions, and user registration was the subject of a request from the Netherlands to Brazil. Dutch authorities were seeking legal assistance in a money laundering investigation involving some 56 Brazilian nationals who were operating tourism agencies and a currency exchange service to conceal proceeds of drug- and corruption-related crime. It has been estimated that some USD 300 million were transferred between 2004 and 2006 by these individuals through offshore accounts to conceal the accounts' true owner and obstruct criminal investigations. Using article 18 as the legal basis made it possible to obtain information relevant to the prosecution and eventually led to the closing of the First Curaçao

63 *Décision 2015–1: Sociéte Orach Placement S-A et Sociéte Fontabel Trading S.A. c/ Direction des Services Judiciaries.*

64 *Sociéte Orach Placement S-A et Sociéte Fontabel Trading S.A. c/ Ministere Public*, Cour de revision, 3 March 2016.

65 McClean, *Transnational Organized Crime*, 210.

International Bank in the Netherlands Antilles, where many of the accounts were held.[66]

A drug trafficking case involving cooperation between Costa Rica, El Salvador, Guatemala concerned an organized criminal group that operated an unregistered freight company offering transportation services between these Central American States and Mexico. The vehicles used were registered to "straw men" acting as subsidiaries to conceal any link to the main company. Between 2004 and 2008, authorities in Costa Rica and Nicaragua made seven separate interceptions, thus confiscating a total of 3,800 kilograms of cocaine and money of a value totalling USD 2,219,000. On the basis of the UNTOC along with *United Nations Convention against Illicit Traffic in Narcotic Drugs and Psychotropic Substances*,[67] authorities sought mutual legal assistance to obtain a range of documents. Several accused later faced criminal charges relating to drug trafficking, conspiracy and criminal association, participation in an organized criminal group, and for various customs offences before a court in San Miguel, El Salvador.[68]

2.4 *Providing Copies of Documents and Records*

Article 18(3)(f) makes specific mention of mutual legal assistance requests for the purpose of obtaining certain official documents and financial transaction records. This subsection needs to be read in conjunction with article 18(8) which mandates that States Parties "shall not decline to render mutual legal assistance pursuant to this article on the basis of banking secrecy". It has been argued that article 18(8) applies regardless of whether there are other binding mutual legal assistance treaties between the requesting and requested States and that banking secrecy must not be used as a ground to decline mutual legal assistance requests if the case falls within the scope of the Convention, even if such refusal is permitted as a ground for refusal of assistance under the other treaty.[69]

Bank records and financial transactions reports were part of a request for mutual legal assistance by the United States to Egypt on the basis of the UNTOC

66 UNODC SHERLOC Case Law Database, case identifier BRAx005 <https://sherloc.unodc.org/cld/case-law-doc/moneylaunderingcrimetype/bra/operation_curaccao.html?lng=en&tmpl=sherloc> (accessed 20 November 2020).

67 Opened for signature 20 December 1988, 1582 UNTS 95 (entered into force 11 November 1990).

68 UNODC SHERLOC Case Law Database, case identifier SLVx001 <https://sherloc.unodc.org/cld/case-law-doc/drugcrimetype/slv/caso_elena.html?lng=en&tmpl=sherloc> (accessed 20 November 2020).

69 McClean, *Transnational Organized Crime*, 215–216; UNODC, *Legislative Guide*, [563].

and the Treaty between the Government of the United States of America and the Government of the Arab Republic of Egypt on Mutual Legal Assistance in Criminal Matters. In this case, some 43 offenders created websites pretending to belong to financial institutions in the US and then sent emails to clients of those institutions asking them to update their personal information. The data obtained from clients who responded to these emails was then used to access their bank accounts and transfer funds into bank accounts held by other participants who then transferred the funds to Egypt. A total of USD 1,117 million was fraudulently acquired this way.[70] US authorities later requested assistance from Egypt to obtain evidence stored on digital devices kept by the persons under investigation as well as records and data from internet service providers in Egypt. The Attorney-General of Egypt accepted the request and instructed its execution.[71]

3 Confiscation

Article 12(1) requires States Parties to adopt measures to enable the confiscation of proceeds and property, equipment, or other instrumentalities used in or destined for offences covered by UNTOC. Article 12 further obligates States to adopt measures to enable the identification, tracing, freezing, and seizing of items for the purpose of eventual confiscation. Article 13(1) requires States Parties that receive a request for confiscation from another State Party to take one of two actions: the requested State must either directly submit, for enforcement by its competent authorities, an order issued by the requesting party (article 13(1)(b)), or else submit the request to its competent authorities in order to obtain a domestic order of confiscation, to which the requested State would be required to give effect if granted (article 13(1)(a)).

The UNTOC has been used on numerous occasions to enable the confiscation or recovery of assets in another jurisdiction. Most of the reported cases involve the registration or execution of foreign restraint orders (or freezing orders as they are sometimes called).

A foreign restraint order was the subject of proceedings before the Court of Appeal in London following a criminal investigation by Kuwaiti authorities into two accused who were husband and wife.[72] The first accused (the husband) had been the Director-General of the Public Institution for Social

---

70 UN Doc CTOC/COP/2010/CRP.5, 3 [7]–[9].

71 UN Doc CTOC/COP/2010/CRP.5, 3 [7]–[9].

72 *A & A v The Director of Public Prosecutions* [2016] EWCA Crim 96.

Security for many years. He allegedly skimmed "commission payments" from an investment fund for which he was responsible. These payments, amounting to several hundred million dollars, were deposited into bank accounts in Switzerland, the United Kingdom, and elsewhere. The second accused (the wife) allegedly assisted in the concealment, movement, and laundering of these funds. The assets the couple had deposited in Switzerland were restrained by Kuwaiti authorities following extensive litigation in Swiss courts.[73] The information gained as a result of this litigation led to further investigations, including an investigation of the assets held by the accused in the UK. Kuwaiti authorities sent a letter of request for legal assistance pursuant to the UNTOC and the *United Convention against Corruption* to the UK in February 2015, followed by a supplementary letter a month later. The letter stated that the accused had been under investigation in Kuwait since 2008 for theft of public funds and money laundering and requested restraint of the accused's assets in the UK.[74] In 2016, the accused appealed against a decision of the Crown Court to issue a restraint order against their assets. The order had been applied for by the Director of Public Prosecutions, acting under the *Proceeds of Crime Act 2002 (External Requests and Orders) Order 2005* and pursuant to the letters of request sent by Kuwait. The Court of Appeal rejected the appeal and the restraint order was upheld.

4 Other Forms of International Cooperation

4.1 *Transfer of Criminal Proceedings*

Article 21 of the UNTOC contains provisions designed to encourage the transfer of criminal proceedings for the prosecution of offences under the Convention. For this purpose, the two States involved first need to evaluate whether the receiving State in which the proceedings are to be held has jurisdiction over the principal issues of the case. Next, the two States need to share and transfer information and evidence and then, if the matter has already reached the courts in one State, it will be necessary to "stay" or suspend the prosecution, pending resolution in the other State.[75]

Only one case could be identified which makes reference to the transfer of criminal proceedings on the basis of article 21. It involved two Dutch nationals

73 Ibid, [14]–[17].

74 Ibid, [19]–[24].

75 UNODC, *Legislative Guide*, [606].

who were accused of drug trafficking.[76] Proceedings that were originally instigated against the two persons by the prosecutor's office in Przemysl, Poland, were later transferred to the competent authorities in the Netherlands. It appears that the UNTOC was the sole basis of this transfer, since Poland is not a Party to the *European Convention on the Transfer of Proceedings in Criminal Matters*.[77]

4.2 *Joint Investigations*

Article 19 of the UNTOC encourages States Parties "to conclude bilateral or multilateral agreements or arrangements whereby, in relation to matters that are the subject of investigations, prosecutions or judicial proceedings in one or more States, the competent authorities concerned may establish joint investigative bodies".[78]

One example of joint investigations carried out on the basis of article 19 involves a collaboration between Brazilian, Portuguese, and Spanish authorities in the investigation of an organized criminal group engaged in trafficking cocaine from Brazil via Portugal to Spain.[79] Spanish and Brazilian authorities provided information to facilitate the investigation led by Portugal. Requests to obtain information on the commercial activities of the main suspect and of companies run by him were also sent to China, Italy, Sweden, Switzerland, the United Kingdom, and the United States. Furthermore, Portugal sent letters rogatory asking Brazilian, Spanish, and US authorities to conduct searches of private homes and offices, interview suspects and witnesses, record property associated with the suspect, and seize bank account deposits. Joint investigative teams were created to intercept phone conversations, conduct surveillance and searches, and seize assets. The suspect was eventually convicted on charges of aggravated drug trafficking and sentenced to 14 years imprisonment. All seized assets were confiscated. On appeal, the Supremo Tribunal de Justica reduced the sentence to 11 years imprisonment.[80]

---

76 UN Doc CTOC/COP/2010/CRP.5, 6 [24].

77 Opened for signature 15 May 1972, ETS No 73 (entry into force 30 March 1978).

78 See further Stefano Betti, "New prospects for inter-state co-operation in criminal matters: The Palermo Convention," *International Criminal Law Review* 3 (2003): 157–158.

79 UNODC SHERLOC Case Law Database, case identifier PRTx002 <https://sherloc.unodc.org/cld/case-law-doc/drugcrimetype/prt/2012/processo_n._142502.2japrt.html?lng=en&tmpl=sherloc> (accessed 12 November 2020).

80 UNODC SHERLOC Case Law Database, case identifier PRTx002 <https://sherloc.unodc.org/cld/case-law-doc/drugcrimetype/prt/2012/processo_n._142502.2japrt.html?lng=en&tmpl=sherloc> (accessed 12 November 2020).

5 Observations

The UNTOC has been used as a legal basis for international cooperation in a myriad of cases. Most of them involve requests for mutual legal assistance under article 18. This may be explained by the broad scope of article 18 and the many types of assistance that may be requested under this provision. Furthermore, many requests are made at the investigative rather than the trial stage of criminal proceedings, which explains the greater number of cases in this category. Boister has similarly noted that the reason why more requests involve mutual legal assistance than extradition is because mutual legal assistance "is in practice usually a precedent to the extradition, it is usually cheaper, and it is less administratively burdensome or likely to engage as much judicial supervision."[81] Because extradition may involve the transfer or prosecution of a person, States generally impose further conditions on making and granting such requests. This may explain the lower number of cases under article 16 compared to cases under article 18.

Other forms of international cooperation under the Convention appear to be rarely used in practice. The possible reasons for this are manifold and may relate, inter alia, to the fact that some of these measures involve the trial or post-trial stage and that some measures are relatively new. Some States may thus be hesitant to use tools of international cooperation with which they have little or no experience, for which they lack applicable domestic laws, and where they may fear that delays or mistakes using such cooperation can jeopardise criminal proceedings.

While this article shows that the UNTOC has been used a legal basis for international cooperation by States around the world, it also reveals that the Convention appears to be far more "popular" among some States than others. The high number of cases reported by Latin American and Caribbean States and States in the "Western European and Others" regional group vis-à-vis the relative paucity of cases from the African and Asia-Pacific regions is noticeable. The administrative, human, and financial resources associated with international cooperation can pose a particular challenge for developing nations and small States, which may explain the lack of reported cases from some States Parties. States in transition and those with scarce resources often experience difficulties in implementing, executing, and enforcing the international conventions they are expected to comply with. For these States, it is particularly important that they benefit from integrated technical assistance activities that focus on building their overall investigation and prosecution capacity as well

81 See also Boister, "Cooperation Provisions," 61.

as their ability to cooperate effectively as envisaged by article 29(3) and (4) of the UNTOC.[82]

This article also demonstrates that the existence of a solid legal basis alone is not sufficient to promote international cooperation on a wider scale. The UNODC's 2012 *Digest of Organized Crime Cases* similarly noted that difficulties in international cooperation do not originate from deficiencies in legal systems but instead from domestic criminal policy and general strategic attitudes: (a) lack of willingness to get involved in a crime that occurred in another country ("your crime is not my crime"); (b) lack of understanding of local criminal phenomena […]; (c) insufficient crime awareness; (d) non-compliance with international legal instruments; and (e) conflicting perceptions of priority issues at the global and regional level.[83]

Despite considerable progress made since the inception of the UNTOC, international cooperation in the investigation and prosecution of transnational organized crime needs considerable strengthening. The many obstacles that still exist to international cooperation in criminal matters include sovereignty issues, the diversity of law enforcement structures, the absence of enabling legislation, a lack of channels of communication for the exchange of information, and divergences in approaches and priorities. These problems are often compounded by difficulties in dealing with the varied procedural requirements of each jurisdiction, the competitive attitude that often exists between the agencies involved, language barriers, and human rights and privacy issues.[84]

The existing regime of international cooperation in criminal matters is still in need of major improvements in order to avoid legislative loopholes and eliminate safe havens. There are still numerous obstacles to quick and predictable cooperation and many processes at international and domestic levels remain opaque and in need of streamlining.[85]

---

82 UNODC, *Criminal Justice*, 2; see further Tomoya Obokata, "The Value of International Law in Combating Transnational Organized Crime in the Asia-Pacific," *Asian Journal of International Law* 7 (2017): 50–51.

83 UNODC, *Digest of organized crime cases* (New York: United Nations, 2012), 54 [112].

84 UNODC, *Criminal Justice*, 2.

85 Ibid, 8.

Status of Implementation of the United Nations Trafficking in Persons Protocol 20 Years after the Palermo Convention

*Fabrizio Sarrica**

Abstract

The fight against human trafficking is still one of the most important and demanding challenges for the United Nations. The international community has made significant progress in combating this criminal phenomenon. This has translated into an overall increase in the number of countries with a proper anti-trafficking legislation and an increase in the number of victims detected and traffickers convicted. Twenty years after the adoption of the Protocol, this paper aims to review the progress accomplished and assess future prospects.

Keywords

human trafficking – UNODC – implementation of measures to combat international crime

1 Introduction: Trafficking in Persons and the United Nations Protocol on Trafficking in Persons

Human trafficking is a crime that ruthlessly exploits women, children and men for numerous purposes including – but not limited to – forced labour and sexual exploitation. In a concerted effort to fight this crime, in November 2000 the United Nations General Assembly adopted the Protocol to Prevent, Suppress and Punish Trafficking in Persons, Especially Women and Children,

* Team leader of the UNODC Research Team on Trafficking in Persons and Smuggling of Migrants and lead author of the UNODC Global Report on Trafficking in Persons.

The views expressed herein are those of the author and do not necessarily reflect the views of the United Nations.

 | DOI:10.1163/9789004469051_004

supplementing the United Nations Convention against Transnational Organized Crime[1] (hereinafter the Protocol). The Protocol entered into force on the 25th of December 2003 and received immediate support from UN Member States: in 2010 there were 137 States Parties, while at the time of writing the States Parties amounted to 178.

Its adoption marked a fundamental step for the international community in combating this form of organized crime: the Protocol differs from other previous international instruments and was the first attempt to reach a "universal agreement addressing all aspects of trafficking in persons",[2] in the awareness that "effective action to prevent and combat trafficking in persons"[3] "requires a comprehensive international approach in countries of origin, transit, and destination".[4]

Human trafficking warrants, in fact, a forceful response founded on assistance and protection for victims, rigorous enforcement by the criminal justice system in order to punish offenders, a sound migration policy to prevent international trafficking and a firm regulation of labour markets.

Twenty years later, the time has come for an evaluation of the level of implementation of the Protocol, with the aim of identifying strengths and weaknesses of this valuable instrument.

Measuring trafficking on the one hand and the success and/or the impact of anti-trafficking policies on the other is not an easy task.[5] Even though the Protocol has helped in harmonizing regional and national legislations by virtue of its widespread ratification and enabled remarkable improvements in the availability of data over the years, significant knowledge gaps remain with regard to the scope of the phenomenon globally as well as the magnitude of the profits made by traffickers, which should make the international community even more concerned about this global crime.

Moreover, recent research shows that difficulties in obtaining accurate and reliable data are often coupled with a weak capacity of countering this crime.[6]

---

1 Protocol to Prevent, Suppress and Punish Trafficking in Persons, Especially Women and Children, Supplementing the United Nations Convention against Transnational Organized Crime, 15 November 2000, UNGA Res. 55/25.

2 Preamble of the Protocol.

3 Idem.

4 Idem.

5 For further information: Ernesto Savona and Sonia Stefanizzi, *Measuring Human Trafficking – Complexities and Pitfalls* (Springer 2007); Kristiina Kangaspunta, "Measuring the Immeasurable: Can Severity of Human Trafficking Be Ranked", *Criminology and Public Policy* 9 (2010): 257–265; Fabrizio Sarrica, "Measuring Trafficking in persons", *Forum on Crime and Society* (2012): 3–17.

6 UNODC, *Global Report on Trafficking in Persons*, 2018, p. 15.

That is why reliable information on the offenders, the victims, and the trafficking flows throughout the world is needed if governments are to achieve long-term successes in combating trafficking in persons.

After a brief introduction to the legal definition of trafficking as provided for by the Protocol and to the patterns of trafficking worldwide, this article will seek to outline the status of implementation of the Protocol, with particular reference to the status of legislation and the criminal justice response.

2 What Is Trafficking in Persons?

One of the major changes introduced by the Protocol is the provision of an agreed definition of trafficking. The purpose behind a universal definition was to facilitate convergence in national approaches to the introduction of trafficking as a domestic criminal offence. Under the Protocol, trafficking in persons can be understood as a process by which people are recruited in their community and exploited by traffickers using deception and/or some form of coercion for this purpose.

The Protocol gives a tripartite definition of trafficking in persons,[7] where trafficking should be understood as:

- the act of "recruitment, transportation, transfer, harbouring or receipt of persons";
- by means of "threat or use of force or other forms of coercion, of abduction, of fraud, of deception, of the abuse of power or of a position of vulnerability or of the giving or receiving of payments or benefits to achieve the consent of a person having control over another person";
- for the purpose of exploitation.

With the only exception of cases involving children,[8] all the aforementioned elements must be present in order for there to be a trafficking in persons offence, although each element has a range of manifestations. These terms are in fact not necessarily precise from a legal point of view and may be defined differently by different jurisdictions, thus broadening or restricting the scope of application of the Protocol. In particular, with regard to the purpose of this crime, article 3 of the Protocol specifies that these forms are – at a minimum – "the exploitation of the prostitution of others or other forms of sexual

7 Art. 3 of the Protocol.

8 Art. 3 c) of the Protocol clarifies that "The recruitment. transportation, transfer, harbouring or receipt of a child for the purpose of exploitation shall be considered 'trafficking in persons' even if this does not involve any of the means" set forth in article 3 a).

exploitation, forced labour or services, slavery or practices similar to slavery, servitude or the removal of organs".[9] The fact that the legal definition sets a minimum threshold has allowed an expansion of the notion of exploitation considered by national authorities, as it has come to include trafficking for the purposes of forced begging, forced marriages, criminal activity, benefit frauds and many others.[10]

Moreover, trafficking in persons need not necessarily be carried out by criminal organizations, nor does it have to be transnational in order to be defined as such in national law.[11]

This means that adjudicated trafficking crimes can look very different from one country to the next. If we couple this with the fact that trafficking in persons affects nearly every country in the world, the complexity of the trafficking crime appears evident. Trafficking in persons is a *complex* crime that manifests itself in a myriad of ways across the world.

3 Main Patterns of Trafficking in Persons

Research conducted by UNODC attempts to shed light on the most prevalent forms of trafficking in persons worldwide.[12] The 2020 edition of the Global Report on Trafficking in Person shows that most of the victims detected across the world are females: mainly adult women, but also increasingly girls.[13] The vast majority of the detected victims of trafficking for sexual exploitation are females, and about one third of the victims trafficked for forced labour are also

9 Art. 3, (a) of the Protocol.

10 Silvia Scarpa, *Trafficking in human beings: modern slavery*, 2008; Anne T. Gallagher, *The international law of human trafficking*, (Cambridge University Press, 2010; Louise Shelley, *Human trafficking: a global perspective*, Cambridge University Press, 2010); Jean Allain, *Slavery in international law: of human exploitation and trafficking*, (Nijhoff, 2012); Ryszard Piotrowicz, Conny Rijken and Baerbel Heide, *Routledge handbook of human trafficking* (Routledge, 2018).

11 Whereas art. 4 of the Protocol specifies that the scope of application thereof extends "except as otherwise stated herein, to the prevention, investigation and prosecution of the offences established in accordance with article 5 of this Protocol, where those offences are transnational in nature and involve an organized criminal group, as well as to the protection of victims of such offences." The Legislative Guide For The United Nations Convention Against Transnational Organized Crime (Palermo Convention) clarifies that "In the case of trafficking in persons, domestic offences should apply even where transnationality and the involvement of organized criminal groups do not exist," 258 para. 25.

12 See UNODC, Global Report on Trafficking in Persons 2006, 2009, 2012, 2014, 2016, 2018 and 2020.

13 See UNODC Global Report, 2020.

females, both women and girls. At the same time, more than half of the victims of trafficking for forced labour are men.

There are considerable regional differences in the sex and age profiles of detected trafficking victims, however.[14] In West Africa, most of the detected victims are children, both boys and girls, while in South Asia, victims are equally reported to be men, women and children. Eastern Europe and Central Asia, a larger share of adult men is detected compared to other regions, while in Central America and the Caribbean, more girls are recorded.

Most of the victims detected globally are trafficked for sexual exploitation, although this pattern is not consistent across all regions. Trafficking of females – both women and girls – for sexual exploitation prevails in the areas where most of the victims are detected: the Americas, Europe, and East Asia and the Pacific.[15] In Central America and the Caribbean, more girls are detected as victims of trafficking for sexual exploitation, while women are more commonly detected as victims of this form of exploitation in the other subregions. Trafficking for forced labour is the most widely detected form in sub-Saharan Africa. In the Middle East, forced labour is also the main form of trafficking detected and mainly involves adults. In Eastern Europe and Central Asia and South Asia, trafficking for forced labour and sexual exploitation are near-equally detected, although with different victim profiles. Apart from sexual exploitation and forced labour, the UN Global Report shows that the ultimate purpose of trafficking can vary regionally.[16] Trafficking for forced marriage, for example, is more commonly detected in parts of South-East Asia, while trafficking of children for illegal adoption is recorded predominantly in Central and South American countries. Trafficking for forced criminality is mainly reported in Western and Southern Europe, while trafficking for organ removal is primarily detected in North Africa, Central and South-Eastern Europe, and Eastern Europe. Many other forms, such as trafficking for exploitation in begging or for the production of pornographic material, are reported in different parts of the world. The detection of other forms of trafficking may partly reflect the ways in which countries have chosen to criminalize different forms of exploitation.

As for the victims of trafficking, the profile of the offenders likewise shows a wide range of different patterns.[17] In some cases the traffickers exploit their own partners; these are cases with criminal dynamics more similar to domestic

14 Ibid, 37.
15 Ibid, 36.
16 Ibid, 36.
17 Ibid, p. 37.

violence than to the activities of mafia-type organizations. In other cases traffickers exploit their own children. In still other cases, trafficking in persons takes the form of communitarian traditions; these include phenomenon such as *les enfants bouvier* (child cowherds), *talibé* children, some forms of forced marriages and many others. In some cases, especially in developed countries, traffickers are organized criminal groups operating across countries. These groups may be organized to a greater or lesser extent, at times reaching the point of being structured like 'mafia-type' criminal organizations.

While large organizations can move a large number of victims for a long period of time, their trade being mainly directed to the more profitable markets in the rich countries in Western Europe and North America, countries in the developing world are mainly affected by internal trafficking, where victims are recruited and exploited in their own countries.[18]

4 United Nations Protocol on Trafficking in Persons

As for the UN Transnational Organized Crime Convention, the intention behind the adoption of the Protocol was to facilitate cooperation among national authorities and civil society, as well as to favour the standardization of national approaches with regard to the establishment of domestic criminal offences that would support efficient international cooperation in investigating and prosecuting trafficking in persons cases. The aim of the Protocol is not limited to enhancing prosecutions and the broader criminal justice response. An additional objective of the Protocol is to "protect and assist the victims of such trafficking, with full respect for their human rights."[19]

In this regard, articles 6, 7 and 8 of the Protocol are focused on the rights of the victims of trafficking, from the right to privacy to the right to housing, legal counselling, medical and psychological assistance, employment, education and training opportunities, as well as compensation for the damage suffered. The Trafficking Protocol goes beyond the aim of providing assistance to the victims of crime. It includes specific provisions on the legal status of the victim, when he or she is a migrant; these provisions are designed to support the introduction of temporary or permanent residence permits. At the same time, the victim is entitled to be repatriated to and received by the country of origin if he or she is willing to go back home.

---

18 According to the UNODC Global Report on Trafficking in Persons 2020, more than 60 per cent of the victims of trafficking worldwide are trafficked domestically.

19 Art. 2 of the UN Protocol.

As noted above, the Protocol has reached almost universal ratification. Any assessment of the status of implementation, however, requires a more specific and detailed analysis of how governments are actually taking actions to prevent the crime, assist the victims and prosecute the traffickers. To this end we must go beyond what government authorities have put down on paper, such as the State's political adherence to an international convention, and assess with measurable indicators how much is being done by them to confront this criminal phenomenon. Over the last decade, the research department of UNODC has been conducting global research with the aim of assessing, among other things, the response of national authorities in their efforts to combat human trafficking. The results of this assessment are published every two years in the UNODC Global Report on Trafficking in Persons.

5 The UNODC Global Reports on Trafficking in Persons

Immediately after the entry into force of the Protocol it was clear that collecting reliable data was vital in the fight against trafficking. The lack of systematic information should not be invoked as a 'justification for inaction' by States Party to the Protocol.[20] The first attempts to fill the gaps date back to April 2006,[21] but it was not until 2010 that the UN General Assembly adopted the UN Global Plan of Action,[22] whereby it requested UNODC to collect information and report biennially on patterns and flows of trafficking in persons at the national, regional and international levels. Such knowledge was necessary, according to the UN General Assembly, for the purpose of sharing "best practices and lessons learned from various initiatives and mechanisms".[23] The mandate marked the launching by UNODC of a series of global reports on trafficking in persons, published in 2012, 2014, 2016, 2018 and 2020.

---

20 See the UNODC Report: Trafficking in Persons Global Patterns, April 2006, where on page 10 it is stated: "Complaining that accurate statistics are difficult to come by may sound like an excuse."

21 The first UNODC Report Trafficking in Persons, Global Patterns was published in April 2006. This report was followed by the 2009 UNODC Global Report on Trafficking in Persons, which was drawn up on the basis of a study conducted by UNODC on the state of the world's response to the crime of human trafficking. These two reports were published before the adoption, by the UN General Assembly, of the UN Global Plan of Action which gave UNODC a mandate to collect information and report biennially on trafficking.

22 United Nations Global Plan of Action to Combat Trafficking in Persons, UNGA Res. 64/293 para. 60.

23 United Nations Global Plan of Action to Combat Trafficking in Persons, UNGA Res. 64/293 para. 60.

Research by UN organizations like UNODC enables us to obtain a global overview of the crime of trafficking in persons across the world. From an international perspective, and with data from many Member States in all regions of the world, it is possible to discern whether certain trafficking patterns or forms of exploitation are more prevalent in some areas, and whether certain trafficking flows are becoming more or less pronounced. In this respect, such information also has the potential to enhance responses at a national level as well as international cooperation in this area.

The Global Report on Trafficking in Persons is intended to fulfil the mandate assigned by the General Assembly, where the aim is to gain basic knowledge with regard to trafficking in persons in order to facilitate the creation and implementation of evidence-based policy interventions.

The data collection for the Global Report on Trafficking in Persons has a dual objective: to achieve the broadest possible geographical coverage while using the most solid information available. While broad geographical coverage is crucial for a report that is global in scope, the solidity of the information is equally important as UNODC's intention is to produce a report that is reliable and accurate.

The information is collected by UNODC in two ways: through a short, dedicated questionnaire distributed every year to governments and the collection of official information available in the public domain (national police reports, Ministry of Justice reports, national trafficking in persons reports, etc.). All the information collected, regardless of source or method, is shared with national authorities for verification prior to publication of this report.

Over the years, UNODC has managed to achieve good coverage – ranging between 130 and 150countries and territories – for the different editions of the Report it has issued. Countries that are not covered are the ones that did not respond to the questionnaire, and in addition, for which UNODC research efforts to locate official national data on trafficking in persons did not yield any results. Official statistics from national authorities account for about 90 per cent of the information collected for the different editions of the Global Report. The remaining 10 per cent is information originating from intergovernmental organizations and non-governmental organizations.

The information collected for the production of the Global Reports includes the number and characteristics of the trafficking cases detected by national authorities; how many victims were detected, the forms of exploitation they were trafficked for, their age, sex and citizenship; how many traffickers, their age, sex and citizenship and the level of the criminal proceedings they are involved in – investigation, prosecution or conviction. These indicators provide a basic overview of the patterns and flows of trafficking in persons at the global, regional and national levels.

At the moment of writing, UNODC had information on about 350,000 victims of trafficking detected between 2003 and 2019 for more than 100 countries around the world. Similar numbers are recorded for traffickers prosecuted and convicted. This makes UNODC the largest depository of trafficking data worldwide. The relevance of the dataset lies, among other things, in its ability to track trends over the years. This information is used to assess progress in the response to trafficking in persons.

6 Status of Implementation: The Legislation Worldwide

At the time of the entry into force of the Protocol, only 33 countries among those assessed in the UNODC 2009 Global Report[24] had legislation in place criminalizing trafficking in persons which was in line with the definition of trafficking given in the UN Trafficking Protocol. That is, legislation targeting all types of exploitation listed in the definition of trafficking and criminalizing the trafficking of adults and children, males and females, as well as cross-border and domestic trafficking. At that time, about 60 per cent of the countries worldwide did not have any specific provisions criminalizing trafficking in persons. It is likely that in these countries other types of criminal offences were used to prosecute traffickers, such as aiding and abetting slavery or trading in slaves. The use of other offences, however, did not allow victims of trafficking to benefit from the rights listed in the Protocol, nor did it enable the national authorities to proceed with requests to other countries for cooperation.

By December 2003, another 41 countries had criminalized only some aspects of trafficking. The countries having a 'partial' legislation belonged to different regions with different legislative legacies; African countries typically only focused on child trafficking, Asian countries tended to criminalize only trafficking of female victims, while Latin American countries had legislation focusing on cross border trafficking, ignoring victims recruited and exploited within the national borders as a form of trafficking. The entry into force of the Protocol resulted in several laws being introduced in a large number of countries. Between December 2003 and November 2008, 64 additional countries introduced specific provisions criminalizing trafficking in persons in line with the Protocol definition of the offence. In November 2008, thirty-five countries still had a specific offence of trafficking in persons restricted to certain forms

24 The total number of countries covered by the 2009 Global Report was 155.

of exploitation and certain categories of victims (e.g. trafficking for sexual exploitation, child trafficking) or without a clear definition of the offence. Around one fourth of the world still did not have any specific human trafficking offence in their legislation as of November 2008. Most of these countries were African or Middle Eastern countries or small island states in the Caribbean or the Pacific. The number of countries introducing the specific offence of trafficking in persons has increased over last decade, with waves of new legislation introduced in Africa and the Middle East. As of August 2020, the vast majority of countries around the world had legislation in place criminalizing trafficking in persons as defined in the Protocol; only a few countries did not have specific laws criminalizing human trafficking, while some populous countries in Asia still defined this crime only in reference to the sexual exploitation or trafficking of women and girls.[25]

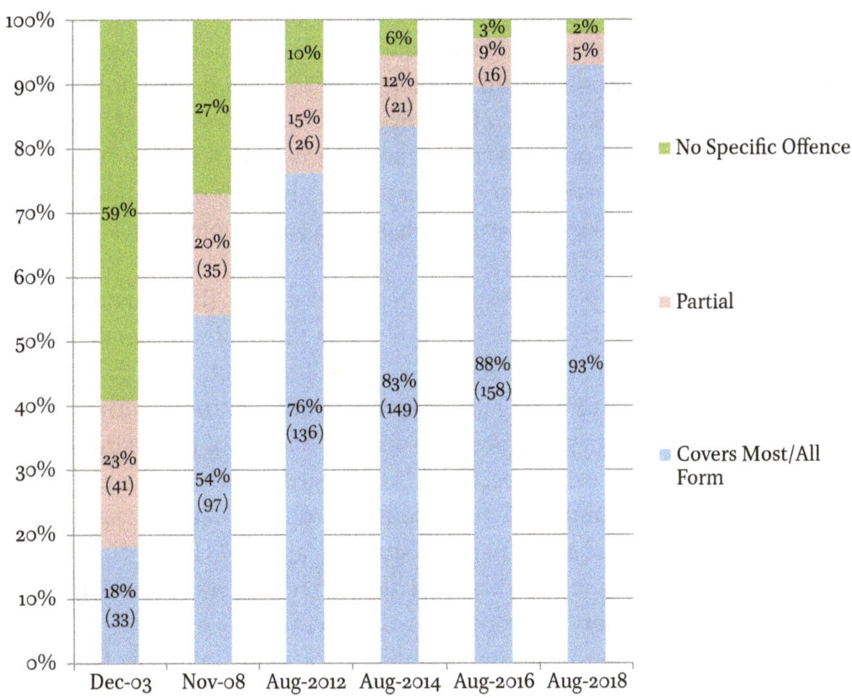

ILLUSTRATION 1 Criminalization of trafficking in persons as a specific offence covering all or some forms of trafficking in persons (TiP) as defined in the UN Trafficking in Persons Protocol, shares of countries 2003–2020, (181 countries)
SOURCE: UNODC ELABORATION ON NATIONAL INFORMAMATION

25 See UNODC Global Report on Trafficking in Persons 2018, 45.

7 Status of Implementation: Criminal Justice Response, Level of Convictions

For (too) many years the criminal justice response to trafficking in persons stagnated at a very low level. During the four years following the entry into force of the UN Trafficking in Persons Protocol, the number of prosecutions and convictions recorded in a large part of the world was very limited.[26] About 40 per cent of the countries assessed in the UNODC Global Report on Trafficking in Persons did not record a single conviction for this crime. An additional 17 per cent of the countries considered recorded less than 10 convictions per year. These data reflect the situation of total impunity traffickers enjoyed in a large part of the world at that time. This impunity was even more acute in Africa, where less than 50 convictions were recorded in the entire continent up to the end of 2007. During those years, the European continent recorded higher conviction rates compared to developing countries. However, in most European countries the recorded national conviction rates for human trafficking was below one person convicted per 100,000 people. In order to contextualize the conviction rates for human trafficking, rates for other crimes may be considered. In Europe, there are more convictions for rare crimes such as kidnapping in Denmark (3 per 100,000 people), homicide in Finland (4 per 100,000 people) or robbery in Norway (5.8 per 100,000 people) than for human trafficking.

The weak criminal justice response recorded during the years after the entry into force of the UN Trafficking in Persons Protocol was mainly due to the absence of legislation or to the fairly recent introduction of most of the legislation addressing trafficking in persons in many countries. As an increasing number of countries introduced the specific offence of trafficking in persons, more convictions were expected to be recorded. In a trend analysis study, UNODC assessed the number of convictions recorded between 2007 and 2010. A few years after the first assessment the situation appeared to have improved; only 16 per cent of the countries assessed did not record a single conviction for trafficking in persons between 2007 and 2010. Over the years, the international community reported an increasing number of cases of trafficking that concluded with a conviction.

In 2020, more than ten years after the first Global Report, a trend analysis on the number of trafficking convictions showed that, globally, they had

26 UNODC Global Report, 2020, 62.

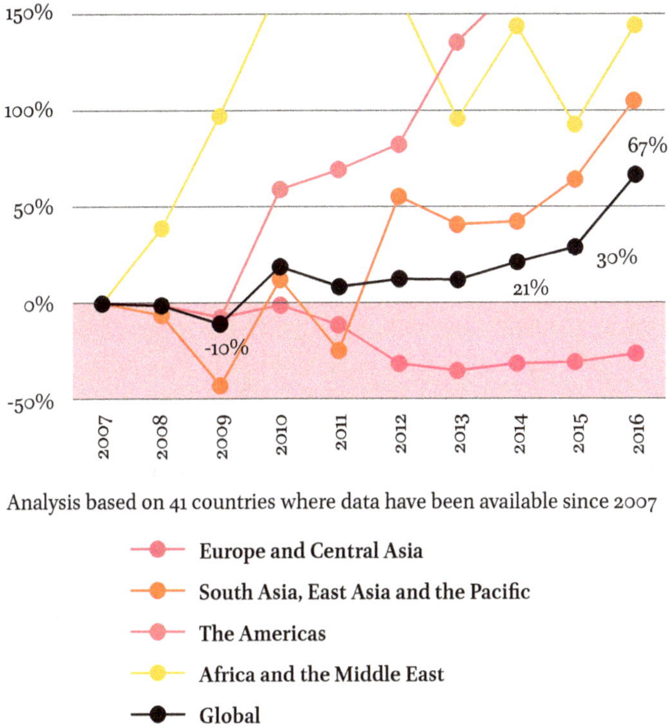

ILLUSTRATION 2 Trends in the number of people convicted of trafficking in persons since 2007 – globally and by region, 2007–2016
SOURCE: UNODC ELABORATION ON NATIONAL DATA

clearly increased over the previous decade.[27] This was true also for most subregions; still today, however, in some parts of the world, even though the trend is increasing, the absolute numbers of convictions remain very low. There appears to be hardly any risk of traffickers facing justice. Many African and Middle Eastern countries have gone from no convictions to a handful of convictions per year in recent years. Consequently, while these countries show a clearly increasing trend, the total numbers in these areas remain very low. European countries, by contrast, report fewer convictions than in the past, but the absolute numbers are still the highest in the world.

The increase in the number of convictions goes hand in hand with the increase in the number of victims detected. The more cases come to light, the more traffickers face justice. Consequently, more victims are detected

27 Ibid.

and – according to the UN Trafficking Protocol – should be assisted. A detailed trend analysis conducted on 45 countries selected in different parts of the world shows that in 2016, about 40 per cent more victims were detected compared to 2011. The most relevant increasing trends were recorded in Asia and the Americas. This is also reflected in the numbers recorded by UNODC when compiling the Global Report on Trafficking in Persons. Year after year, UNODC has increased the number of victims detected included in the UNODC database. This is due on one hand to an increased coverage of the countries providing information, and on the other hand to an increase in the number of detections per country covered. Countries are identifying more victims; in 2016, on average, each country detected 254 victims, while in 2010 this number was 150.

For many of the countries that have recorded increasing trends in convictions or the detection of victims, the institutional responses are related to this increase. In particular, in more than 40 countries recording some increase in the number of detected victims between 2003 and 2016, anti-trafficking measures were introduced by the State authorities shortly before the increases occurred; for instance, the introduction of new anti-trafficking legislation or an amendment to existing legislation resulted in an increase in the number of victims detected in many countries, from Kuwait to Paraguay, from Nigeria to the United Arab Emirates. The implementation of the Anti-Trafficking National Action Plan in Nepal in 2012[28] was followed by a sharp increase in the detection of trafficking victims. Similar examples can be found in many countries around the world; however, the putting in place of a National Action Plan, the establishment of a Rapporteur or the creation of a national prosecution body specialized in human trafficking does not always result in better anti trafficking performances.

The difference between a successful and a weak anti-trafficking response probably lies in the training of personnel, the number of people involved, cooperation between institutions and the available budget, as well as many other factors that could be summarized into two categories: capacity and institutional will. It does not come as a surprise that the areas of the world that are weaker in combating trafficking are the developing countries. There are exceptions, however, both in negative and positive terms.

In order to assess the institutional capacity of the States parties, UNODC conducted an analysis based on information from 107 countries and territories that reported information on the number of convictions as well as victims

28 National Plan of Action Against Trafficking in Persons 2068 (2012).

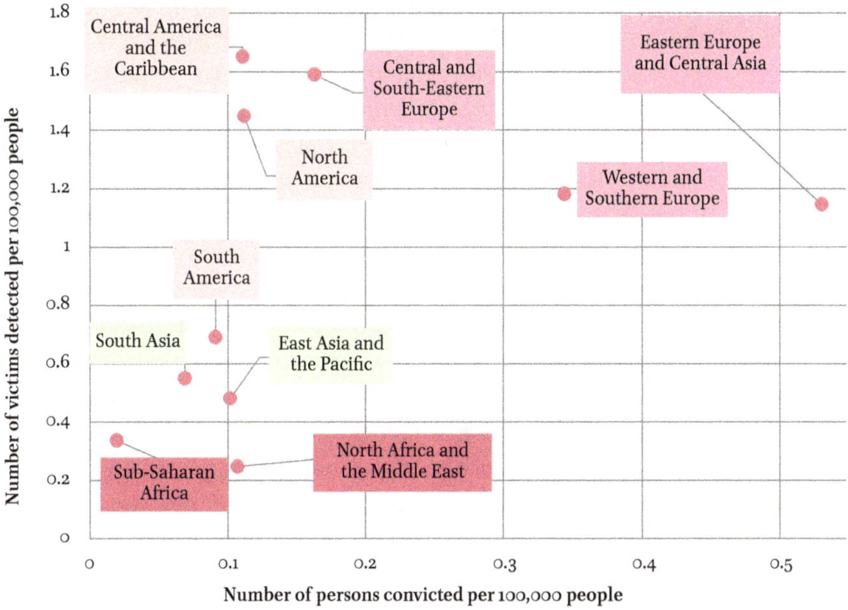

ILLUSTRATION 3 Subregions by average number of trafficking convictions and number of victims detected per 100,000 population, 2014-2017

detected during the period 2014–2016. In order to avoid bias in terms of a country's population, UNODC measured how many traffickers were convicted and how many victims were detected per 100,000 people. These two numbers were divided by the countries' populations. The resulting indicators were placed in a Cartesian coordinate system in order to graphically represent how the different world's regions were performing in detecting victims (vertical axis) and convicting traffickers (horizontal axis).

The countries near the top-right corner of the graph are the ones detecting the most victims and convicting the most traffickers: in short, the ones recording a high response to the offence. The countries at the bottom left are the countries recording the lowest responses.

According to this analysis, the countries performing the best are located in Europe and include both Western and Eastern European countries, which record on average between 0.35 and 0.55 convictions, and detect about 1.2 victims per 100,000 people. Countries in Sub-Saharan Africa record about 0.02 convictions per 100,000 people and detect about 0.3 victims per 100,000 people.

Countries in North Africa and the Middle East are, on average, convicting more but detecting less victims than other regions. Asian countries, on average, are performing better than Africa and the Middle East, but much worse than Europe and the Americas. In the Western Hemisphere, North and Central American countries are performing better than South American countries. In greater detail, North and Central American countries are detecting more victims compared to the rest of the world. This may due to the use of looser criteria for defining 'victims' of trafficking; some countries wait for cases to conclude with a conviction before counting a victim, whereas others differentiate between the criminal proceedings and the victim referral and assistance process.

The analysis confirms that large areas of impunity still exist in some parts of the world. In sub-Saharan Africa and in some parts of Asia, the rates of both detected victims and convicted offenders are low compared to other regions. At the same time, these regions are the most frequently the origin of human trafficking, as may be seen when we look at cross-border and long-distance trafficking. Victims from these two subregions are detected in a larger number of destination countries than victims from other regions of origin. In addition, while most trafficking flows originate and are detected within the same subregion, the vast majority of trafficking victims detected in other regions come from East Asia or sub-Saharan Africa.

This suggests that a lower capacity to detect trafficking cases, and thus to convict the traffickers, results in a failure to provide justice to victims. In addition, impunity creates an incentive for traffickers to operate and broaden their illegal activities.

8 Conclusions – 20 Years on the Path against Human Trafficking

In modern times, the path taken by the international community in order to combat trafficking can be summarized in some important milestones.

The negotiation and subsequent adoption of a legally binding instrument with an agreed definition of trafficking in persons, such as the one contained in the Protocol, was the starting point for efficient international cooperation among different national authorities. The Protocol, like the Transnational Organized Crime Convention, was intended to promote international cooperation in investigating and prosecuting cases of trafficking in persons. Furthermore, considering the specificities of the crime considered, an additional objective of the Protocol is to protect and assist trafficking victims while ensuring full respect for their human rights. This must be consistent at the national level as well as across borders. In order to achieve this, harmonized implementation of the Protocol is needed.

In July 2010, a few years after the entry into force of the Protocol, the international community signed another important document on the fight against trafficking in persons: the General Assembly approved the Global Plan of Action to Combat Trafficking in Persons.

This General Assembly resolution was intended to be more operative, for instance by creating a trust fund[29] for victims of trafficking in persons, currently managed by UNODC, with the aim of supporting local NGOs in assisting victims of trafficking with small grants.

Another concrete activity emerging from the Global Plan of Action to Combat Trafficking in Persons is the biennial UNODC Global Report on Trafficking in Persons. UNODC has been conducting research on trafficking in persons since the year 2000; however, paragraph 60 of the Global Plan of Action entrusts UNODC with the responsibility for collecting data from national authorities in order to monitor the patterns and flows of human trafficking, as well as for sharing best practices in combating trafficking in persons.

The Report is designed for research and analytical purposes. In practice, the Global Report has turned into a highly effective tool for monitoring the implementation of the Protocol. In the context of the Global Report, over the years, UNODC has collected information on the national responses to human trafficking, mainly in terms of the number of traffickers prosecuted and convicted, the number of victims assisted and the number of countries adopting a legislation broadly in line with the Trafficking in Persons Protocol.

The analysis on the status of legislation clearly shows that most Member States introduced legislation in line with the Protocol only after 2003, under the pressure of the Protocol itself. The legislative framework is therefore quite recent. In some parts of the world, like Southern Africa, East Africa, North Africa and some countries of the Middle East and South Asia, the offence of trafficking in persons was only introduced after 2013. Trafficking in persons remains a relatively new crime in many legislations and jurisdictions. This has clearly had an impact on the capacity of investigators, prosecutors and judges to effectively combat trafficking.

Time is needed in order for national institutions to get acquainted with and develop know-how on using all the instruments existing in the United Nations Trafficking in Persons Protocol, from prevention to prosecution, from victim assistance to international cooperation. A learning curve was assessed by UNODC in the UNODC 2014 Global Report on Trafficking in Persons;[30] it shows

29 United Nations Global Plan of Action to Combat Trafficking in Persons, UNGA Res. 64/293, para. 4.

30 UNODC, Global Report on Trafficking in Persons, 2014, 56.

a clear correlation between the length of time a country has had legislation that criminalizes trafficking as required by the Protocol, and the number of convictions for trafficking crimes in that country.

The countries with many convictions were characterized by having enacted Protocol-aligned trafficking legislation earlier than, for instance, Sub-Saharan Africa or the Middle East.

Whereas countries that had legislation in place before the entry into force of the Protocol recorded, on average, about 29 convictions in the year 2014, those that had introduced the offence in the period 2003–2008 had about 18 convictions in the same year. Far fewer convictions were reported by countries that had introduced legislation between 2009 and 2012, and those enacting legislation after 2012 had no convictions in the year 2014.

The new legislative framework can explain why for many years and in different parts of the world, the number of victims identified and assisted were very few for a crime that appears to be extremely widespread. The number of prosecutions and convictions remained greatly limited, allowing human traffickers to operate with impunity in vast parts of the world.

On the other hand, the analysis above can be misleading. The introduction of the offence does not on its own give rise to the action that is required to effectively combat trafficking in persons. Concrete governmental actions have proved to result in more victims being assisted and in more people being convicted a few months after the introduction of such actions. In some countries, well-designed, well-resourced national action plans on trafficking in persons, or the creation of specialized investigative and prosecutorial teams have led to more lives being saved, and these are real obstacles to traffickers' activities.

Like the introduction of the Protocol in 2003, the 2010 Global Plan of Action may have also determined another important push in the direction of adequate implementation of the Protocol. Since 2010, the number of victims detected and traffickers convicted has steadily increased.

Nowadays, almost all countries in the world have introduced the specific offence of trafficking in persons and most of these are Parties to the Protocol. Policies and national responses have been tested. Good practices have emerged over the years. It is time now for these practices to be shared and transformed into standardized protocols, and for the lessons learned to be incorporated into institutional knowledge. The year 2020 – which marks 20 years since the entry into force of the Protocol and ten years since the publication of the United Nations Global Plan of Action to Combat Trafficking in Persons – can be a new milestone along this path toward an adequate response to this crime.

Smuggled Migrants as Victims?

Reflecting on the UN Protocol against Migrant Smuggling and on Its Implementation

*Alessandro Spena**

Abstract

After outlining the UN Protocol's general approach to migrant smuggling, this article raises the question of whether and to what extent smuggled migrants can be said to be victims of this crime. The author argues that an affirmative answer is possible in at least three different respects: smuggled migrants can be victimized by states fighting against migrant smuggling and irregular immigration (secondary victimization); but, of course, they can also be victimized by smugglers (primary victimization), in two ways: first, if smuggling is so performed as to put their lives, physical integrity or dignity at risk; secondly, smugglers also victimize migrants by profiting of their vulnerable condition, and their need to enter a foreign country, in order to gain economic benefit.

Keywords

migrant smuggling – Smuggling of Migrants Protocol – EU Facilitation package – Directive 2002/90/EC

1 Approaches to Migrant Smuggling

There are two main reasons why states may be willing to counter migrant smuggling. The first – which may be called *state-centred* – has to do with migrant smuggling being linked to irregular immigration: although it should be clear that not all smuggled migrants are irregular in the proper sense (many of them being refugees and asylum seekers), smuggling is nonetheless one of the most

* Professor of Criminal Law, University of Palermo.

 | DOI:10.1163/9789004469051_005

conspicuous ways by which irregular immigration takes place; fighting it can thus be, and frequently is, a way for states to fight irregular immigration itself.

A second reason for states to be concerned with migrant smuggling is instead an expression of (what might be called) a *migrant-centred* (or *migrant-sympathetic*) *approach*, stemming from the need to protect migrants themselves from the many risks they may face if smuggled: economic exploitation, deception, degrading treatment along the way, physical injuries and death, not to mention the constant and serious risk for smuggled migrants to fall prey to unscrupulous criminal networks[1] devoted to human trafficking[2] or to kidnapping for ransom.[3]

Each of these two approaches corresponds to a different interpretation of the wrongness of migrant smuggling – of the reason why such conduct deserves social stigmatization and criminalization.

Under a state-centred approach, the wrongness of migrant smuggling is made dependent on the wrongness of irregular immigration, the former activity being a means to achieve the latter, and thus on the assumption that states are entitled to close their borders and select who to admit into their territories. The reason why smuggling is seen as a problem, under this perspective, lies not so much in the relationship between the smuggler and the smuggled migrant, but in the relationship between the smuggled migrant and the foreign state: a relationship in which smugglers are only secondary parties. Migrant smuggling, as a consequence, though formally described as a distinct offence, is in fact criminalized as a kind of *complicity* in the foreigner's irregular immigration, to which smugglers are only seen as accessories, mere facilitators; the

1 Art. 15, par. 2, of the Protocol Against the Smuggling of Migrants by Land, Sea and Air, Supplementing the United Nations Convention Against Transnational Organized Crime (henceforth: Smuggling of Migrants Protocol): "In accordance with article 31 of the Convention, States Parties shall cooperate in the field of public information for the purpose of preventing potential migrants from falling victim to organized criminal groups."

2 On this risk, see, e.g., Smuggling of migrants into, through and from North Africa (unodc 2010, available at: www.unodc.org/documents/human-trafficking/Migrant_smuggling_in_North_Africa_June_2010_ebook_E_09-87293.pdf, last accessed 31 Decembe 2020) Ch. ix; Philippe De Bruycker, Anna Di Bartolomeo and Philippe Fargues, "Migrants smuggled by sea to the EU: Facts, laws and policy options," MPC Research Report, 9/2013, 4 ff. (available at: http://www.migrationpolicycentre.eu/docs/MPC-RR-2013-009.pdf, last accessed 31 December 2020); Smuggled Futures: The dangerous path of a migrant from Africa to Europe, Geneva: Global Initiative against Transnational Organised Crime (Global Initiative against Transnational Organised Crime 2014, available at: www.globalinitiative.net/smuggled-futures/, last accessed 31 December 2020) 7 ff.

3 See Katie Kuschminder and Anna Triandafyllidou, "Smuggling, Trafficking, and Extortion: New Conceptual and Policy Challenges on the Libyan Route to Europe," in *Antipode*, 52 (2020): 206–226.

wrongness of their deed is of a derivative nature, a wrongness that is secondary to the (alleged) primary wrongness of irregular immigration.[4]

In contrast, under a migrant-centred approach, migrant smuggling is conceived, both formally and substantially, as a wrong in itself, independently of the (alleged) wrongness of irregular immigration. Its wrongness, under this perspective, can be seen as a function of the position of *vulnerability* of the smuggled migrant vis-à-vis his/her smuggler: a vulnerability that typically – though not necessarily – manifests itself in the execution of the smuggling deal, as can be easily inferred from the very fact that smugglers' conduct frequently takes place in ways that harm or put at risk the rights of those smuggled (see, e.g., Article 15, paragraph 1, UN Smuggling of Migrants Protocol): their right to life, their right to physical integrity, their right not to be tortured or subjected to inhuman and degrading treatment.

2 The Hybrid Approach of the UN Smuggling of Migrants Protocol

The UN Smuggling of Migrants Protocol underlies a hybrid approach, in which both the state-centred and the migrant-centred perspective are given space, though to a different extent.

According to the statement of purpose, in Article 2, the Protocol's aim "is to prevent and combat the smuggling of migrants, as well as to promote cooperation among States Parties to that end, while protecting the rights of smuggled migrants". On one hand, this provision shows that states are fully aware of the fact that the smuggling of migrants can put at risk the rights of those smuggled and that they consider the protection of these rights one of the aims of the Protocol; on the other hand, however, the grammatical form of the whole sentence (and in particular, the use of the subordinating conjunction "while" to link the fight against migrant smuggling and the protection of smuggled migrants' rights) also suggests that the two aims, though practically linked, are assumed to be conceptually separated: in the logic of this statement, preventing and combating the smuggling of migrants do not per se involve also protecting smuggled migrants; this latter aim is assumed to be at the side of

4 Incidentally, it should be noted that this approach does not require that irregular immigration itself be punished as a crime; even adopting a state-centred approach towards migrant smuggling, states may be willing not to criminalize irregular immigrants as such: due, for instance, to lato sensu humanitarian reasons (based on the awareness of the fact that many smuggled migrants find themselves in very difficult situations) or to reasons of political realism (based, for instance, on the awareness of the low deterrent impact that criminalization has on the decision of migrants to irregularly enter or stay in the territory of foreign states).

("while"), and not intrinsic to, the former. Which brings us back to the state-centred approach and the idea that fighting against migrant smuggling is, first of all, a way of defending the territorial sovereignty of states against irregular immigration.

Articles 3 (definition) and 6 (criminalization) seem to go along the same line (but see *infra*, § 3.4): article 6, paragraph 1(*a*), requires states parties to criminalize the smuggling of migrants, "when committed intentionally and in order to obtain, directly or indirectly, a financial or other material benefit"; article 3(*a*), in its turn, defines "smuggling of migrants" as "the procurement, in order to obtain, directly or indirectly, a financial or other material benefit, of the illegal entry of a person into a State Party of which the person is not a national or a permanent resident" (with article 3(*b*) defining "Illegal entry" as the fact of "crossing borders without complying with the necessary requirements for legal entry into the receiving State"). Neither provision takes into specific consideration the migrants' rights that can be violated in the commission of the crime; these rights are only given relevance in article 6, paragraph 3, as aggravating factors of the crime.

3 The Kaleidoscopic Figure of the Smuggled Migrant

Even though a migrant-sympathetic sensitivity is not alien to the Smuggling of Migrants Protocol, it is not clear exactly what role smuggled migrants are given in it: while the UN Trafficking in Persons Protocol[5] unquestionably treats trafficked persons as victims of traffickers, the Smuggling of Migrants Protocol is much more ambiguous as to whether smuggled migrants are to be considered as victims of smuggling.

3.1 *Smuggled Migrants as Objects of Smuggling*

Throughout the Smuggling of Migrants Protocol smuggled migrants are generally depicted, in practically every provision in which they are mentioned, as "object[*s*] of the conduct" of smugglers, thus being assigned a basically passive role.

Indirectly, this same notion of smuggled migrants as mere "objects of the crime" is confirmed by the definition of the crime of migrant smuggling as "the *procurement*, in order to obtain, directly or indirectly, a financial or other

5 Protocol to Prevent, Suppress and Punish Trafficking in Persons Especially Women and Children, supplementing the United Nations Convention against Transnational Organized Crime.

material benefit, of the illegal entry of a person into a state Party of which the person is not a national or a permanent resident" (article 3(*a*))." Two circumstances are of relevance here. The syntactic structure of the sentence, defining the smuggler's criminal conduct in "causal" terms, as the "procurement" of a result (the irregular entrance of the foreigner), conceptually locates smuggled migrants on the passive side of the deed, their position entering the picture as part of the result of the smuggler's conduct, not as an active contribution to it. This is further confirmed by the fact that the smuggled migrants' position is not described through verbs (e.g., "to assist the foreigner to irregularly *enter* or *stay*"), but through nouns (*entrance, stay*): while verbs describe the performance of an action, nouns have instead the effect of syntactically stressing that smuggled migrants are credited the passive role of being the "objects" of other persons' actions.[6] It is no accident that, during the Protocol's preparatory work, "[o]ne delegation considered the concept of 'procurement of illegal entry' to be problematic. In the view of that delegation, it would be better to make reference to complicity in and aiding and abetting the violation of national migration laws."[7]

A second relevant circumstance is the requirement of the profit motive as a definitional element of crime: if read against the general background of the Palermo Convention against transnational organized crime, this circumstance suggests the idea that, in the logic of the Smuggling of Migrants Protocol, the smuggling of migrants is essentially seen as an activity of transnational criminal organizations aimed at gaining a profit; this implicitly depicts smuggled migrants as mere instruments exploited by others for their own benefit, as subjects taken into consideration not so much for any action they may perform, but because of the mere fact that they represent sources of illicit enrichment of other persons.

Further evidence of the smuggled migrants' passive role within the Smuggling of Migrants Protocol can be found in article 5, which explicitly states that "[m]igrants shall not become liable to criminal prosecution under

6 Alessandro Spena, "Human Smuggling and Irregular Immigration in the EU: From Complicity to Exploitation?," in S. Carrera and E. Guild (eds.), *Irregular Migration, Trafficking and Smuggling of Human Beings* Brussels: CEPS, 2016) 37; Valsamis Mitsilegas, "The Normative Foundations of the Criminalisation of Human Smuggling. Exploring the Fault Lines between European and International Law," in *New Journal of European Criminal Law*, 10, (2019): 68–85.

7 See Travaux préparatoires of the negotiations for the elaboration of the United Nations Convention against Transnational Organized Crime and the Protocols thereto, New York: United Nations, 2006, 464, nt. 2 (available at: https://www.unodc.org/documents/treaties/UNTOC/Publications/Travaux%20Preparatoire/04-60074_ebook-e.pdf).

this Protocol *for the fact of having been the object of conduct* set forth in article 6 of this Protocol." This provision, while restating that smuggled migrants are mere "object[*s*] of conduct", rules out that any criminal liability can derive therefrom. This does not mean, of course, that they cannot be punished for other crimes, the commission of which may be entailed by their being smuggled (typically, the crime of irregular entrance or stay); the rule established in Article 5, however, clarifies that they should not be charged *with the crime of smuggling*, which is exactly a consequence of the fact that their role, in the performance of the action, is merely that of an "object of criminal conduct".

3.2 *Smuggled Migrants as Rights-Holders*

If we go deeper into the Protocol, however, we easily realize that this document does not limit itself to depicting smuggled migrants as passive objects; it also provides them with the active role of *claimants*, rights-bearing subjects deserving protection.[8]

This can already be inferred from several abstract statements in the *Preamble* (where it is declared that states parties are "[c]onvinced of the need to provide migrants with humane treatment *and full protection of their rights*," and "[a]lso concerned that the smuggling of migrants can endanger the lives or security of the migrants involved"), in the *statement of purpose* (with article 2 expressly stating, as seen earlier, that the protection of migrants' rights is one of the Protocol's purposes) and in the *scope of application* (with article 4 establishing that "[t]his Protocol shall apply[…] to the prevention, investigation and prosecution of the offences [*of migrant smuggling*] as well as to the *protection of the rights of persons who have been the object of such offences*").

But the same inspiration can also be found in many other provisions disseminated throughout the Protocol, which depict smuggled migrants not merely as *objects* of conduct, but also as *subjects* of rights: Article 6, paragraph 3 (concerning smuggled migrants' right not to have their life or safety endangered by smugglers and their right not to be treated inhumanly or degradingly by them), article 9 (requiring states, among other things, to "[e]nsure the safety and humane treatment of the persons on board" when boarding and searching suspect vessels according to Article 8), Article 14 (establishing the duty for states to train their officials not only in preventing smuggling but

8 See, among others, Anne T. Gallagher and Fiona David, *The International Law of Migrant Smuggling*, (New York, Cambridge University Press, 2014) Ch. 8; Anne Gallagher, "Whatever Happened to the Migrant Smuggling Protocol?," in Marie McAuliffe and Michele Klein Solomon (Conveners), *Ideas to Inform International Cooperation on Safe, Orderly and Regular Migration*, Geneva: IOM, 2017, 3 f.

also "in the humane treatment of migrants who have been the object of such conduct, *while respecting their rights as set forth in this Protocol*"), Article 16 (requiring the implementation of the Protocol to be constantly attentive to smuggled migrants' rights),[9] Article 18 (requiring that states carry out the return of smuggled migrants *"with due regard for the safety and dignity of the person"* [paragraph 5] and *"without prejudice to any right* afforded" to them "by any domestic law of the receiving State Party" [paragraph 7]), Article 19 (establishing that "[n]othing in this Protocol shall affect the other rights, obligations and responsibilities of States and individuals under international law [...]" [paragraph 1] and "[t]he measures set forth in this Protocol shall be interpreted and applied in a way that is not discriminatory to persons on the ground that they are the object of" smuggling [paragraph 2]).

3.3 *Smuggled Migrants as Victims?*

Such a wide-ranging acknowledgement of smuggled migrants as rights-holders, of course, does not mean *per se* that they are in fact considered as victims of smuggling. Though smuggled migrants are not viewed as co-perpetrators of the criminal conduct, the basic form of the crime, as we already know, seems to be drafted in state-centred terms, as the violation of an interest – the control of migratory flows – of which states, not migrants, are the owners. The *Travaux préparatoires* support this view, by stressing that "[a]t its eleventh session, the Ad Hoc Committee considered, finalized and approved article 3 [*now article 2*], as amended after extensive discussion. The protection of the rights of migrants was again in the forefront of the debate, while it was agreed that the notion of 'victims', as incorporated in the corresponding article of the trafficking in persons protocol, was not appropriate in the context of the present article."

However, we should not be too hasty in drawing the conclusion that in the Smuggling of Migrants Protocol smuggled migrants are utterly denied victimhood under any possible meaning of the word. The fact that they are explicitly

---

9 Each state party, indeed, shall:

a. "take [...] all appropriate measures[...] to preserve and protect the rights of persons who have been" smuggled "as accorded under applicable international law, in particular the right to life and the right not to be subjected to torture or other cruel, inhuman or degrading treatment or punishment" (par. 1);

b. "take appropriate measures to afford migrants appropriate protection against violence that may be inflicted upon them, whether by individuals or groups, by reason of being the object of" smuggling (par. 2) ;

c. "afford appropriate assistance to migrants whose lives or safety are endangered by reason of being the object of" smugglin g;

d. "take into account the special needs of women and children."

treated as rights-holders deserving protection suggests, on the contrary, that there can be situations in which their victimization must be acknowledged.

To better understand how and in what sense this is so, we must begin by making it clear that the rights afforded by the Smuggling of Migrants Protocol to smuggled migrants can be divided into two different categories: some of these rights are directly, though not necessarily, involved in the perpetration of a conduct of smuggling (see Articles: 6, paragraph 3; 15, paragraphs 1 and 2; and 16); others can be involved, instead, in the actions taken by states to prevent and combat migrant smuggling (see Articles: 9; 14; 18, paragraphs 5 and 7; and 19). While, then, in the first case migrants are recognized to have claims (and to deserve protection) against smugglers, in the second case they are recognized to have claims (and to deserve protection) against states, and in particular against those violations that may stem from a rough and unrestrained exercise of states' (alleged) right to fight irregular immigration.

The migrant-sympathetic approach in the Smuggling of Migrants Protocol has, consequently, a twofold dimension, to which, I argue, two possible forms of victimization of smuggled migrants can be traced back. The type of victimization that can be linked to the first category of the aforementioned rights (the right to life; the right not to be subjected to torture or other cruel, inhuman or degrading treatment or punishment; more generally, the right to have no violence inflicted upon oneself) has the effect of *increasing* the wrongness of migrant smuggling in view of the fact that, besides violating the territorial sovereignty of states, it can also violate – at least, in some cases – the interests of those smuggled; as so interpreted, the migrant-sympathetic approach provides *external support* for the state-centred approach: that is, the need to protect migrants' rights adds further reasons against migrant smuggling to the state-centred reason of protecting states' territorial sovereignty; therefore, it supplements the (alleged) value of states' territorial sovereignty with a value system of a different kind (pertaining to the rights of individuals, not of states), which, however, goes in the same direction of supporting the criminalization of migrant smuggling.

This entails a form of *primary victimization* of smuggled migrants,[10] though this does not directly stem from smuggling as such, but rather from the ways in which this conduct can be manifested in practice: a kind of victimization that

10 Primary victimization is victimization stemming from the fact of being the victim of a crime: a primary victim of crime is someone who suffers the harm/wrong described in the definition of that crime. Secondary victimization refers instead to negative – harmful or, at least, traumatic – consequences stemming, for the victim him- or herself (typically in the form of victim blaming or insensitivity), from the process of social control aimed at either preventing or repressing crime.

is not a consequence of the mere fact of having been smuggled, but of some activities that can be – and frequently are (as is expressly acknowledged in Article 15, paragraph 1) – carried out by smugglers in their effort to procure the migrants' irregular entrance or stay in a foreign country. This makes smuggled migrants into victims, not of smuggling in its basic form (Article 6, paragraph 1), but rather of the aggravated forms of the crime (Article 6, paragraph 3).

The possibility of a *secondary victimization* of smuggled migrants stems instead from the recognition that, besides having rights vis-à-vis their smugglers, they also have rights that states may infringe while fighting against smugglers: the right to safety and to be treated humanely (Article 9, paragraph 1(a); Article. 14, paragraph 1; Article 18, paragraph 5); the right not to be discriminated against (Article 19, paragraph 2); and the right to be treated according to "international humanitarian law and international human rights law and, in particular, where applicable, the 1951 Convention and the 1967 Protocol relating to the Status of Refugees and the principle of non-refoulement as contained therein" (paragraph 1). The Smuggling of Migrants Protocol thus conceives of smuggled migrants as *doubly vulnerable* subjects, caught between two fires: they are vulnerable not only to smugglers (who can both endanger their lives or physical safety and treat them inhumanly), but also to states (who can victimize them through actions carried out against smugglers). Under this second perspective, the migrant-sympathetic approach works not so much in support of, but as a *counterpoint* to the state-centred one: it serves to counterbalance it, establishing that smuggled migrants have rights that limit what states can do in pursuing their aim of combating irregular immigration through migrant smuggling.

3.4 *Migrant Smuggling as Exploitation? The Profit Motive*

Now, I want to push my argument further by questioning the idea that smuggled migrants cannot be qualified as primary victims of smuggling as such but only of its aggravated forms: the basic form of migrant smuggling, as defined in the Protocol (Articles 6, paragraph 1(*a*) and 3 (*a*)), I argue, is not exhaustively explained as an expression of the state-centred approach; indeed, there is room for interpreting it in a migrant-oriented perspective, whereby we might see some kind of primary victimization of smuggled migrants reflected in it.

Attention must be drawn to the fact that the Protocol's definition of the crime of smuggling does not revolve exclusively around the procurement of the irregular entry of foreigners into the territory of a State (or their unauthorized stay there), but that it also requires, as we have seen, that this conduct be engaged in "in order to obtain, directly or indirectly, a financial or other material benefit."

Being completely irrelevant to the integrity or violation of state territorial sovereignty, such a "profit motive" has nothing to do with a state-centred approach or with the state's interest in fighting migrant smuggling because it is an avenue for irregular immigration. What, then, is the meaning and purpose of including this element in the definition of the crime? According to the *Travaux préparatoires*,[11] the intention underlying this element is twofold: on one hand, it should be read as an expression of the Protocol being specifically concerned with migrant smuggling as an activity of transnational criminal organizations, based on the assumption that these organizations smuggle migrants as part of their criminal business; on the other hand, the element should also be read as a positive – though implicit – formulation of a humanitarian/familial defence to migrant smuggling, aimed at excluding criminal liability for those acting on the basis of humanitarian or family reasons.

The criminological background of the crime is thus typically represented by the organized action of smugglers aiming to profit from foreigners trying to circumvent the restrictions posed by states to their regular entry and stay. This gives the crime of smuggling an overarching meaning of *exploitation* that supplements the state-centred focus on the smuggler/state relationship with a second focus on the relationship between the smuggler and the smuggled migrant; the definition thus ceases to be exclusively concerned with the procurement of the migrant's irregular entry or stay and starts also being concerned with the conditions under which the smuggling arrangement is agreed upon. The disparity between the position of the smuggler and that of the smuggled person is of relevance here: people resort to smugglers when they find themselves caught between the need or desire to enter a different country than their own, on the one hand, and the unavailability of legal avenues for them to do so, on the other; this puts them in a condition of weakness, which smugglers can take advantage of in order to gain some benefit. The wrongness of migrant smuggling, as thus interpreted, extends beyond the mere violation of state territorial sovereignty, since it also requires that the difficult position of migrants be *exploited* for the sake of profit.

Does this make smuggled/exploited migrants into *victims* of their smugglers? Yes, I would argue, at least in those cases in which migrants resorting

---

11 See Travaux préparatoires, cit., 469: The reference to "a financial or other material benefit" as an element of the definition in subparagraph (a) [of art. 3] was included in order to emphasize that the intention was to include the activities of organized criminal groups acting for profit, but to exclude the activities of those who provided support to migrants for humanitarian reasons or on the basis of close family ties. It was not the intention of the protocol to criminalize the activities of family members or support groups such as religious or non-governmental organizations.

to smugglers find themselves in a *position of vulnerability* of a kind analogous to that of victims of human trafficking. Article 2(2) of Directive 2011/36/EU defines a "position of vulnerability" as "a situation in which the person concerned has no *real* or *acceptable* alternative but to submit to the abuse involved": when migrants have "no *real* or *acceptable* alternative but to submit to" smuggling – for instance, because smuggling is the only way they have to escape from famine, war, torture or persecution – the fact that smugglers exploit their vulnerable condition in order to gain profit can be seen as a wrong committed against them: taking advantage of their vulnerability to secure profit for themselves is a way of victimizing them, even if the smuggling does not concretely involve the use of violence or take place in such a way as to put the migrants' lives or safety at risk.

Importantly, this kind of victimization is specific to smuggling and is not necessarily captured by the criminalization of human trafficking: human trafficking requires, indeed, that the criminal conduct be perpetrated for the purpose of further exploiting the trafficked person, whereas this is in principle irrelevant to migrant smuggling; the wrongness of the exploitation of smuggled migrants is not a function of their fate beyond the foreign state borders, but rather of their being forced to resort to smugglers due to their difficult situation, i.e. of their having no real or acceptable alternative to being exploited by smugglers.

Again, this is a merely *possible* – not a necessary – form of primary victimization, since there can be cases in which migrants resorting to smuggling do not find themselves in a vulnerable position. When, however, smuggled migrants happen to be vulnerable subjects, their exploitation by smugglers makes them into victims of smuggling as such, even though they are smuggled in ways that do not put their lives or physical integrity at risk nor entail that they are treated inhumanly.

4 Intermediate Summary

To recap, the Smuggling of Migrants Protocol reflects a hybrid approach to migrant smuggling, according to which:

- a) the basic form of the crime (Article 3 (a)) is conceived as a violation of states' (alleged) right to restrict the regular entry or stay of foreigners within their territories;
- b) smuggled migrants are depicted as being not so much co-perpetrators, but rather objects of the smugglers' conduct;

  ba) as long as they limit themselves to this role as mere objects, they should not be held criminally liable for smuggling (art. 5);

- c) smuggled migrants are recognized as being entitled to some rights the violation of which amounts to (or should be seen, I argue, as amounting to) victimization (of different types); they are thus recognized as *possible victims* of smuggling;

  ca) some of these rights are held vis-à-vis states and limit their power to prevent and combat smuggling; a violation of these rights would amount to *secondary victimization* of smuggled migrants;

  cb) other rights are held by smuggled migrants vis-à-vis their smugglers and their violation amounts to *primary victimization* of smuggled migrants;

    cba) the first kind of such primary victimization, which can take place during the practical execution of the smuggling arrangement, is expressly addressed by Article 6, paragraph 3, as an aggravating factor ((*a*) endangerment of "the lives or safety of the migrants concerned"; (*b*) "inhuman or degrading treatment, including for exploitation, of such migrants");

    cbb) the second kind of primary victimization could occur, on the other hand, as a result of the smuggling agreement itself, whereby smugglers get paid for their "service" by vulnerable foreigners who need to migrate but have no realistic alternative to do so other than through smuggling; this kind of victimization is not explicitly addressed as such in the Protocol, but it can be inferred by:

      cbba) the fact that the Protocol only criminalizes migrant smuggling performed in order to gain some material benefit;

      cbbb) the fact that the aim of gaining a benefit is tied to the exploitation of the smuggled migrant's condition;

      cbbc) the fact that such exploitation victimizes the migrant if it is an abuse of a position of vulnerability in which the migrant finds him/herself; and

      cbbd) the fact that such victimization would not be covered by the criminalization of human trafficking in those cases in which the smuggling is not aimed at further exploiting the smuggled migrant.

5 Challenges for the Smuggling of Migrants Protocol's Implementation

Now, what about the implementation of the Smuggling of Migrants Protocol? As of today, 150 states have ratified this instrument; less than those that have ratified the Trafficking in Persons Protocol (178), but nonetheless a significant number of ratifications. Notwithstanding this, it could hardly be said that the great bulk of such ratifications also share the hybrid approach which we have seen underlying the Smuggling of Migrants Protocol.[12] During the last fifteen years, states have been particularly inclined to get tougher on migrant smuggling; but they have done this from a basically state-centred perspective, using the fight against migrant smuggling as a means to control (hence, as a form of indirect criminalization of) irregular immigration. The migrant-sympathetic approach pervading the SoM Protocol has been recessive and has remained largely unimplemented.[13]

The European approach against smuggling is a paradigmatic example. The EU ratified the Smuggling of Migrants Protocol in 2006;[14] nevertheless, as of today, the EU legislation on this matter is still based on the so-called *Facilitation package* of 2002 (Directive 2002/90/EC plus Framework decision 2002/946/JHA), which is inspired by a completely different – heavily state-centred – view of migrant smuggling compared to what emerges from the Smuggling of Migrants Protocol.

I have insufficient space to delve deeper into this point here;[15] therefore, I will limit myself to making some quick remarks. Article 1, paragraph 1(*a*), of the Facilitation Directive, describes migrant smuggling (which it emblematically calls "facilitation of irregular immigration") as the fact of "any person who intentionally assists a person who is not a national of a Member State to enter, or transit across, the territory of a Member State in breach of the laws of the State concerned on the entry or transit of aliens." As can be easily grasped: (1) the provision defines conduct not in causal, but rather in complicity terms, as the fact of *assisting* migrants to illegally enter, not as the fact of *causing* their entrance (*facilitation* of irregular entry, transit or stay – not *smuggling*

---

12 See, e.g., Gallagher, "Whatever Happened to the Migrant Smuggling Protocol?": "in implementing their legislative and regulatory responses, States have moved substantially away from the core tenets of the Protocol" (p. 2).

13 On the problems faced by the implementation of the Smuggling of Migrants Protocol, see, in general, Andreas Schloenhardt and Hamish MacDonald, "Barriers to Ratification of the United Nations Protocol Against the Smuggling of Migrants," in *Asian Journal of International Law*, 7 (2017): 13–38.

14 http://ec.europa.eu/word/agreemeents/prepareCreateTreatiesWorkspace/treatiesGeneralData.do?step=0&redirect=true&treatyId=2841, last accessed 31 December 2020.

15 For further reflection, see my "Migrant Smuggling: A Normative and Phenomenological View from Italy", in Vincenzo Militello and Alessandro Spena, *Between Criminalization and Protection. The Italian Way of Dealing with Migrant Smuggling and Trafficking within the European and International Context* (Leiden: Brill, 2019). See also Javier Escobar Veas, "Smuggling of Migrants is and Should be Established as an Autonomous Offence", *European Journal of Crime, Criminal Law and Criminal Justice* 27, (2019): 226 ff.

of migrants); (2) the role of smuggled migrants is consequently worded using verbs (*to enter, to transit across*), not nouns, which suggests the view that the migrants themselves are actively involved in the perpetration of the crime; (3) the criminalization of inward smuggling (facilitation of irregular entry) is not made dependent upon the pursuit of profit (while, by contrast, a profit motive is required when it comes to the facilitation of irregular *stay*: Article 1, paragraph 1(*b*)).

Article 1, paragraph 2, of the Directive, moreover, gives Member States the option of deciding "not to impose sanctions with regard to the behaviour defined in paragraph 1(a) by applying its national law and practice for cases where the aim of the behaviour is to provide humanitarian assistance to the person concerned." This means, however, that Member States are not obliged, but merely permitted to grant "facilitators" acting for humanitarian reasons a humanitarian defence for their conduct. In Member States that have chosen not to avail themselves of this option (such as, for instance, Italy, Portugal and Germany), this puts potential helpers at risk of being criminalized as smugglers, thereby indirectly impacting the situation of migrants in need of help.[16]

16 On so-called "humanitarian smuggling", see, among others, Elspeth Guild and Sergio Carrera (2013), "EU Borders and Their Controls. Preventing unwanted movement of people in Europe?" [2013], ceps Essay (available at: https://www.ceps.eu/system/files/No%206%20EU%20Borders%20and%20their%20Controls%20revised.pdf, last accessed 31 December 2020) 2; Jennifer Allsopp, "The European Facilitation Directive and the Criminalisation of Humanitarian Assistance to Irregular Migrants: Measuring the Impact on the Whole Community," in Sergio Carrera and Elspeth Guild (eds.), *Irregular Migration, Trafficking and Smuggling of Human Beings* (Brussels: CEPS, 2016) 47; Ead., Solidarity, "Smuggling and the European Refugee Crisis: Civil Society and Its Discontents," *Diritto, immigrazione e cittadinanza,* (2017) (https://www.dirittoimmigrazionecittadinanza.it/archivio-saggi-commenti/saggi/fascicolo-n-3-2017/167-saggio-allsopp: last accessed 31 December 2020); Liz Fekete, "Europe: crimes of solidarity", in *Race & Class*, (2009): 83 ff.; Tugba Basaran, "The saved and the drowned: Governing indifference in the name of security," *Security Dialogue* (2015) 7 ff.; Liz Fekete, Frances Webber and Anya Edmond-Pettitt (eds.), *Humanitarianism: The Unacceptable Face of Solidarity* (London: Institute for Race Relations, 2017) (https://s3-eu-west-2.amazonaws.com/wpmedia.outlandish.com/irr/2017/11/10092853/Humanitarianism_the_unacceptable_face_of_solidarity.pdf: last accessed, last accessed 31 December 2020); Rachel Landry, "Decriminalising 'Humanitarian Smuggling'", RSC Research in Brief 6, March 2017 (https://www.rsc.ox.ac.uk/publications/research-in-brief-decriminalising-humanitarian-smuggling, last accessed 31 December 2020); Sergio Carrera *et al., Policing Humanitarianism. Eu Policies Against Human Smuggling and their Impact on Civil Society* (Oxford-London: Hart, 2019); Alessandro Spena, "Smuggling umanitario e scriminanti", *Rivista italiana di diritto e procedura penale*, 4 (2019).

Many EU states follow the same track as the EU Facilitation Package, though in different forms and to a different extent.[17] The reasons why this is so can be easily guessed. Firstly, from a nomodynamic perspective, EU directives are more binding for EU states than UN conventions and protocols, the implementation of which is largely contingent upon the will of states themselves. Secondly, from a historical-political perspective, a decisive role can be attributed to the fact that the state-centred approach emerging from the Facilitation Package is particularly attuned to the natural propensity of states to prioritize their own interests (such as the interest in migration control) and those of their own citizens over the interests of foreign nationals. Moreover, European states conceive themselves more as countries of immigration than as countries of emigration, which makes them much more sensitive to the problems (allegedly) raised by uncontrolled immigration than to those faced by foreigners leaving their homeland in search of a better life.

Such a prevalently state-centred approach falls short of implementing the SoM Protocol: the lack of a profit-driven element in the definition of the crime of smuggling, coupled with the insufficient relevance given to humanitarian reasons, excessively widens the scope of the criminalization of migrant smuggling; while giving pre-eminence to states' interest in controlling their borders, this also results in an indirect criminalization of those who are smuggled, to the prejudice of the rights whose protection is among the Protocol's fundamental aims.

17 For a comparative survey focused on Italy, Portugal, Spain and Germany, see Alessandro Spena, "L'incriminazione dello smuggling of migrants in Europa: una ricognizione comparatistica", in Vincenzo Militello *et al.* (eds.), *Traffici illeciti nel Mediterraneo. Persone, stupefacenti, tabacco* (Turin: Giappichelli, 2019) 141–163.

Protocol against the Illicit Manufacturing of and Trafficking in Firearms, Their Parts and Components and Ammunition

Implementation Challenges and Responses

*Simonetta Grassi**

Abstract

This article gives an overview of the thrust and core provisions of the Protocol against the Illicit Manufacturing of and Trafficking in Firearms, Their Parts and Components and Ammunition 20 years after its adoption. It examines the interlinkages between illicit firearms trafficking and other crimes and the ability of the Firearms Protocol to address these threats, as well as its ties to other international instruments in this area and existing challenges and responses in its implementation.

Keywords

Firearms Protocol – illicit firearms trafficking – Sustainable Development

Introduction

On 13 November 2015 in Paris, terrorists killed 130 people with illicitly trafficked firearms, whilst another 413 were wounded. The terroristic attack shed light on the shadow world of illicit firearms trafficking.

The present article gives an overview of the thrust and core provisions of the Protocol against the Illicit Manufacturing of and Trafficking in Firearms, Their Parts and Components and Ammunition (Firearms Protocol)[1] 20 years after its

* Head of the Global Firearms Programme, UNODC.

1 United Nations, Protocol against the Illicit Manufacturing of and Trafficking in Firearms, Their Parts and Components and Ammunition, supplementing the United Nations Convention against Transnational Organized Crime, A/RES/55/255 of 31 May 2001.

 | DOI:10.1163/9789004469051_006

adoption. It examines the interlinkages between illicit firearms trafficking and other crimes and the ability of the Firearms Protocol to address these threats, as well as its ties to other international instruments in this area and existing challenges and responses in its implementation.

1 Framing the Issue of Illicit Trafficking in Firearms

Illicit firearms trafficking is not only a serious crime in itself, but it is often also linked to other serious offences, whose negative impact and harmful effects are aggravated by the presence and use of illicit firearms, such as drug and human trafficking, other forms of transnational organized crime, gang criminality or terrorism. The availability of firearms, their parts and components, and ammunition to organized criminal and terrorist groups exponentially increases their destructive power, facilitates the commitment of violent crimes and – as a lucrative trafficking commodity – provides them with financial means to pursue their goals and to perpetuate their power. Illicit firearms cause insecurity, fuel and prolong conflicts and, as also recognized by the 2030 Agenda for Sustainable Development, constitute an impediment to sustainable development.

According to the United Nations Office on Drugs and Crime (UNODC) Global Homicide Study of 2019, 54 % of the reported homicides in 2017 were committed with a gun. In the Americas, this figure rises up to nearly three quarters of all homicides – one quarter of all homicides reported worldwide that year.[2] The majority of these crimes appear to be closely associated with the illicit drug trade and other forms of organized crime. The Mexican drug war alone caused an estimated death-toll of 200,000 to 250,000 persons between 2006 and 2018.

In Africa, the fall of the Gaddafi regime and the widespread proliferation of weapons from its arsenals have contributed to the militarization of several terrorist groups, especially in the wider Maghreb and Sahel regions, where significant amounts of weapons were trafficked from Libya through Niger to supply firepower to armed groups in northern Mali from 2011 to 2013. However, this route reversed from 2014 onwards, when the power vacuum created after Gaddafi's death led Libya into a civil war, increasing internal demand and producing a counter flow of ammunition and firearms back to Libya.[3]

2 UNODC, *Global Study on Homicide 2019*, (Vienna, 2019) Booklet 1, 19.

3 Fiona Mangan and Matthias Nowak (Small Arms Survey), *The West Africa – Sahel Connection, Mapping Cross-border Arms Trafficking* (Geneva 2019), 5 f.

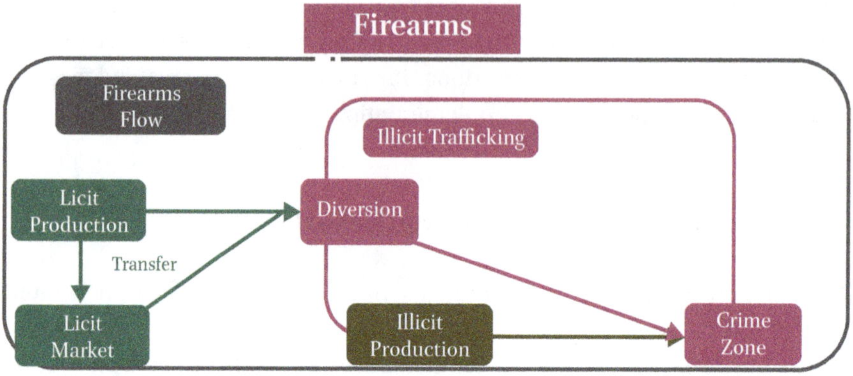

FIGURE 1 Legal and illicit firearms flows

The above examples show the interconnectedness between firearms trafficking, organized crime and terrorism. However, their role in criminal investigations is often neglected. Firearms trafficking remains one of the most invisible and unresolved crimes: not only are illicitly trafficked firearms most often only detected after the trafficking has taken place, at the moment of their use in criminal or terroristic activities, but even when its illicit nature is apparent, too often criminal investigations focus on the crime committed with the firearm, rather than also investigating its illicit origin and supply chain.

However, countering firearms trafficking presents multiple challenges, as we will see further below. One major reason for these challenges is linked to the fact that the vast majority of firearms were legally manufactured to begin with and later diverted into the grey and black markets, thus producing a complex interplay between two mutually influencing arms markets: the legal one and the illicit one.

The modalities through which firearms enter the black markets are manifold and complex. Diversion can occur at any time in their lifecycle: at the time of manufacture, or when held in national stocks, they can be stolen or lost if not properly accounted for or secured; they can be diverted from dealers or civilian owners, including private security companies, through straw purchases, thefts or losses, or illegal sales; diversion can occur at the time of transfer to a non-authorized destination, or final end use or end user, or in violation of embargoes. Other modalities include the illegal conversion, assembly or production of firearms, parts and components in violation of national laws and international treaties.

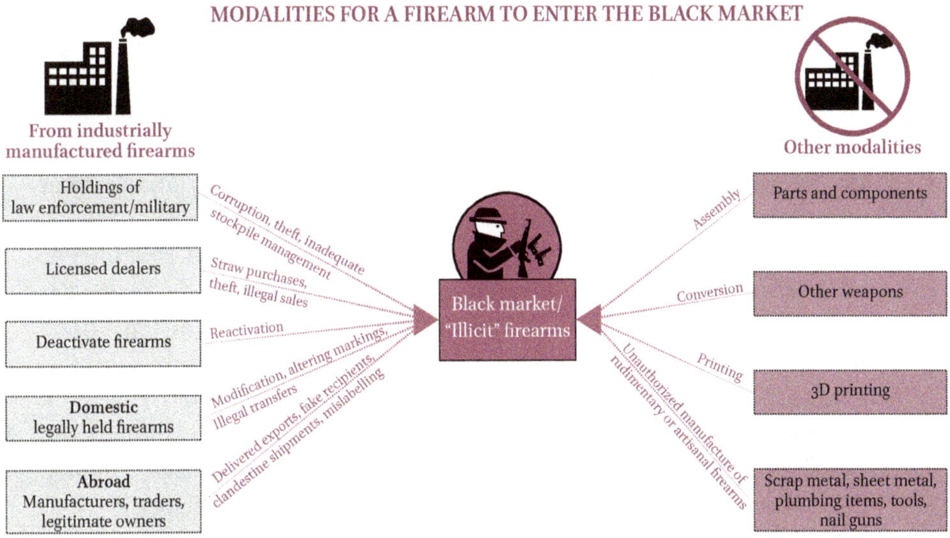

FIGURE 2 Modalities of diversion. UNODC's Global Study on Firearms 2020

2 Addressing Illicit Firearms Trafficking at a Policy Level[4]

2.1 *The International Framework on Firearms Control*

The Firearms Protocol was adopted on 31 May 2001 by the General Assembly, as the third protocol supplementing the United Nations Convention against Transnational Organized Crime – known as the Organized Crime or Palermo Convention or UNTOC.[5] The Organized Crime Convention together with the Firearms Protocol, the Protocol to Prevent, Suppress and Punish Trafficking in Persons, Especially Women and Children and the Protocol against the Smuggling of Migrants by Land, Sea and Air, represents the commitment of the international community to counter transnational organized crime. Finally entering into force on 3 July 2005, the Firearms Protocol was the first international legally binding instrument related to firearms and, as a significant achievement, the only instrument so far that has required the illicit

4 For a comprehensive overview of the international legal framework related to small arms see UNODC, *The Firearms Protocol and the Arms Trade Treaty: Divergence or Complementarity?* (Vienna 2016); Sarah Parker and Marcus Wilson, *A Guide to the UN Small Arms Process – 2016 Update*, 3rd ed. (Geneva: Small Arms Survey, 2016).

5 United Nations General Assembly, "United Nations Convention against Transnational Organized Crime", A/RES/55/25 of 15 November 2000.

manufacturing of and trafficking in firearms, their parts and components, and ammunition,[6] as well as the tampering with markings, to be established as criminal offences. The implementation of the Organized Crime Convention and its supplementing protocols will be incentivized by the expected adoption of a review mechanism during the Conference of the Parties in October 2020. In a peer-to-peer process, this mechanism allows States Parties to jointly review the implementation progress in detail.

The history of the Firearms Protocol dates back to 1995 and is intimately linked to the context of efforts to address transnational organized crime under the auspices of the Economic and Social Council (ECOSOC) of the United Nations and its Commission on Crime Prevention and Criminal Justice. The basis for the work on the Protocol was the Inter-American Convention against the Illicit Manufacturing of and Trafficking in Firearms, Ammunition, Explosives, and Other Related Materials – known as CIFTA – which was adopted on 14 November 1997 and was at that time the only existing agreement.[7]

According to Article 2 of the Firearms Protocol, the purpose of the Protocol "is to promote, facilitate and strengthen cooperation among States Parties in order to prevent, combat and eradicate the illicit manufacturing of and trafficking in firearms, their parts and components and ammunition." As the provisions of the parent Organized Crime Convention apply to the Firearms Protocol, mutatis mutandis, this purpose must be read in conjunction with the purpose of the Organized Crime Convention (Article 1 of the Convention), "to promote cooperation to prevent and combat transnational organized crime more effectively." In this overall context, the Firearms Protocol aims to prevent and control illicit activities commonly involving firearms that are associated with transnational organized crime groups. It seeks to do so by providing a framework to control and regulate the manufacture of firearms and legal arms flows, prevent their diversion into the illicit market, and facilitate the investigation and prosecution of related offences without hampering legitimate transfers. Its implementation process is overseen by UNODC in Vienna.

The Firearms Protocol is part of a larger construct of international and regional,[8] partly overlapping and certainly complementary, legal instruments

---

6 In the context of the Firearms Protocol, the term "firearms, their parts and components, and ammunition" will be hereinafter referred to as "firearms", if not expressly mentioned.

7 OAS, "Inter-American Convention against the Illicit Manufacturing of and Trafficking in Firearms, Ammunition, Explosives, and Other Related Materials ('CIFTA')", AG/RES.1 (XXIVE/97) of 14 November 1997.

8 See as prominent examples the Inter-American Convention against the Illicit Manufacturing of and Trafficking in Firearms, Ammunition, Explosives, and Other Related Materials ('CIFTA'), AG/RES.1 (XXIVE/97) of 14 November 1997; the Central African Convention for the

that have mutually influenced and reinforced each other and provided a framework aimed at interrupting the illicit flow of firearms. The Firearms Protocol must be read also in the light and as a part of this overarching framework. The common starting point in the adoption of these instruments was the acknowledgement that firearms are not per se an illicit commodity and that each State is entitled to manufacture, import and retain firearms for its self-defense and security needs, and the establishment of specific responsibilities and duties of States to control these arms and prevent them from falling into the hands of criminals or other unauthorized persons. Moreover, building on the assumption that most firearms were legally manufactured and diverted into the grey and black market at some time during their lifecycle, the instruments address the issue from different, but complementary angles.

At the international level, two political documents and one international treaty complement the Firearms Protocol and its parent Convention:

The legally non-binding *Programme of Action to Prevent, Combat and Eradicate the Illicit Trade in Small Arms and Light Weapons in All Its Aspects* of 2001[9] – known as the Programme of Action or PoA – and the *International Instrument to Enable States to Identify and Trace, in a Timely and Reliable Manner, Illicit Small Arms and Light Weapons* of 2005[10] – known as the International Tracing Instrument or ITI – were negotiated in the context of disarmament and arms control, under the auspices of the First Committee of the General Assembly, which deals with disarmament and international security. However, the scope of the two political documents is not limited to disarmament, but rather includes a broad set of recommended measures and actions at the national, regional and international levels, ranging from the regulation of ownership and possession, to criminal justice responses, effective and secure stockpile management, brokering controls, marking, record keeping and tracing as well as arms trade regulation, the establishment of national commissions on small arms and light weapons and the promotion of

Control of Small Arms and Light Weapons, their Ammunition and All Parts and Components that can be used for their Manufacture, Repair and Assembly of 30 April 2010; the Protocol on the Control of Firearms, Ammunition and other Related Materials in the Southern African Development Community (SADC) Region of 14 August 2001; DIRECTIVE (EU) 2017/853 OF THE EUROPEAN PARLIAMENT AND OF THE COUNCIL of 17 May 2017 amending Council Directive 91/477/EEC on control of the acquisition and possession of weapons.

9 United Nations, Programme of Action to Prevent, Combat and Eradicate the Illicit Trade in Small Arms and Light Weapons in All Its Aspects, A/CONF.192/15 of 20 July 2001.

10 United Nations, International Instrument to Enable States to Identify and Trace, in a Timely and Reliable Manner, Illicit Small Arms and Light Weapons, A/60/88 of 27 June 2005.

civil society engagements. The PoA, in particular, does not contain any legally binding provisions or definitions. It rather offers a broad and inclusive framework for action, which leaves it up to Member States to decide on whether and how to implement the recommended measures. The ITI, on the other hand, focuses on the tracing of firearms/SALW and provides for measures and good practices to promote cooperation in international tracing requests, building on the UNTOC and Firearms Protocol provisions on international cooperation.

In 2013, the international community adopted the second global instrument focusing on the regulation of international trade in conventional arms, including small arms and light weapons. The Arms Trade Treaty (ATT),[11] which entered into force in 2014, establishes legally binding commitments. In order to prevent and eradicate the illicit trade in such arms and prevent their diversion (Article 1 of the ATT), States Parties undertake to govern their export, import, transit, trans-shipment and brokering. The centrepiece of the Arms Trade Treaty is a set of detailed arms export licensing criteria, set forth in Articles 6 and 7 of the treaty, which follow a phased approach of prohibitions and export assessment. Under Article 6 the export of conventional arms, including small arms and light weapons, must be prohibited if the transfer would violate United Nations Security Council arms embargos, if the exporting State party would violate its relevant international obligations under international agreements, or if the State Party has knowledge that the arms would be used in the commission of, inter alia, crimes against humanity, war crimes or attacks directed against civilian. Where the requirements for such a prohibition do not apply, States Parties are obliged to conduct a risk assessment, taking into account a set of criteria set forth in Article 7(1). States Parties must assess the potential that the arms would undermine peace and security, or could be used to commit or facilitate a serious violation of international humanitarian or human rights law, or an act constituting an offence under international conventions or protocols relating to terrorism and transnational organized crime. If the exporting State Party determines that there is an overriding risk of any of the aforementioned negative consequences, it must not authorize the export (Article 7(3) of the ATT).

The reference to the Firearms Protocol in Article 7(1) (b) (iv) of the Arms Trade Treaty shows the interconnected system of the international framework related to firearms and brings us back to the original topic of this article.

11 United Nations, Arms Trade Treaty, A/CONF.217/2013/L.3 of 27 March 2013.

2.2 *Firearms in the Context of Sustainable Development and Security*

With the adoption of the 2030 Agenda for Sustainable Development in 2015, which succeeded the Millennium Development Goals of 2000, the General Assembly recognized the devasting impact of firearms on sustainable development and security.[12] At the heart of the 2030 Agenda are the 17 Sustainable Development Goals, which are an urgent call for action by all countries. Sustainable Development Goal 16 is to "promote peaceful and inclusive societies for sustainable development, provide access to justice for all and build effective, accountable and inclusive institutions at all levels". Among its 10 associated targets, target 16.4 aims to "significantly reduce illicit financial and arms flows, strengthen the recovery and return of stolen assets and combat all forms of organized crime" by 2030. The final text of the target acknowledges that illicit financial and arms flows can constitute a form of organized crime in themselves, but at the same time they enable, interconnect and fuel various forms of organized crime; and that the reduction of such flows goes hand in hand with combatting organized crime in general.

With regard to global security, the United Nations Security Council, in its resolution 2370 (2017)[13] on Preventing Terrorists from Acquiring Weapons, acknowledged the nexus between illicit firearms trafficking, organized crime and terrorism. In the resolution, the Security Council stated that it was gravely concerned that "the illicit transfer, destabilizing accumulation and misuse of small arms and light weapons in many regions of the world continue to pose threats to international peace and security, causes significant loss of life, contribute to instability and insecurity" and was "strongly condemning the continued flow of weapons, including small arms and light weapons, [...] to and between [terroristic organizations], their affiliates, and associated groups, illegal armed groups and criminals, and encouraging Member States to prevent and disrupt procurement networks for such weapons". Furthermore, the Security Council referred to core provisions of the Firearms Protocol by recognizing:

> the need for Member States to undertake appropriate measures consistent with international law to address the illicit trafficking in small arms

---

12 United Nations General Assembly, Transforming our world: the 2030 Agenda for Sustainable Development, A/RES/70/1 of 21 October 2015.

13 United Nations Security Council, Threats to international peace and security caused by terrorist acts – Preventing terrorists from acquiring weapons, S/RES/2370 (2017) of 2 August 2017.

and light weapons, in particular to terrorists, including by enhancing, where appropriate and consistent with their domestic legal frameworks, national systems for collection and analysis of detailed data on illicit trafficking of such weapons to terrorists, and putting in place, where they do not exist, adequate laws, regulations and administrative procedures to exercise effective control over the production, export, import, brokering, transit or retransfer of small arms and light weapons within their areas of jurisdiction, taking into consideration the "Programme of Action to Prevent, Combat and Eradicate the Illicit Trade in Small Arms and Light Weapons in All Its Aspects" in order to prevent the illicit trafficking to terrorists of such weapons.

2.3 *Structure and Core Provisions of the Firearms Protocol*[14]

The Firearms Protocol itself combines preventive measures with substantive criminal law as well as investigative and prosecutorial approaches. Pursuant to Article 4(1), the Protocol is intended to apply "to the *prevention* of illicit manufacturing of and trafficking in firearms, their parts and components and ammunition and to the *investigation and prosecution of offences*_established in accordance with [the] Protocol where those offences are transnational in nature and involve an organized criminal group." An in-depth interpretation shows an interesting division in the scope of application of preventive and criminalization measures. The two qualifiers, "transnational in nature" and the involvement of "an organized criminal group", apply to the investigation and prosecution of firearms-related offences only, not to the prevention of such offences. The limitation of the scope of application regarding investigation and prosecution is a manifestation of the interplay between the parent Organized Crime Convention and the supplementing Firearms Protocol. As the provisions of the Firearms Protocol must be read in conjunction with the scope of application of the Organized Crime Convention pursuant to Article 3(1), the qualifier that the convention will apply only where the offence is transnational in nature and involves and organized criminal group also limits the scope of application of the supplementing Firearms Protocol. However, despite the limitation of those qualifiers on investigation and prosecution, Member States acknowledged that, in order to prevent illicit trafficking and manufacturing, a State must establish a regulatory system with broad application that allows it

14 For a detailed analysis see Legislative Guides for the Implementation of the United Nations Convention Against Transnational Organized Crime and the Protocols Thereto, (United Nations publication, 2014), 425 ff.

to control any firearm on its territory at any time during its lifecycle, irrespective of transnational links.

2.3.1 Preventive and Security Measures

The central policy of the Firearms Protocol is to control and ensure the traceability of firearms, their parts and components and ammunition, to control their cross-border movement and to criminalize any transaction or transfer that does not comply with the requirements of the Protocol.

The Protocol provides for a comprehensive and reciprocal system for the import, export and transit of firearms, their parts and components and ammunition, requiring States to provide authorizations to one another before permitting shipments of firearms to leave, arrive in or transit across their territory and enables law enforcement to track the legal movement of shipments to prevent theft and diversion (Article 10). These standards are intended to help ensure a level of transparency such as to enable States Parties to better target illicit transactions. Measures designed to control manufacturing are also included.

Linked to manufacturing and to the import/export/transit regime is the recording and marking of firearms. Both domestic and international efforts to reduce illicit trafficking rest on the ability to track and trace individual firearms. That, in turn, requires firearms to be uniquely identified and recorded. One of the law enforcement tools in the Protocol, therefore, is the marking of firearms at the time of manufacture, import and transfer from government stocks, when disposal other than destruction occurs and when a firearm is deactivated (Articles 8, 9 and 6(2)). Also, records must be kept in order to support later tracing based on the information generated by marking the firearms and the issuance of authorizations (Article 7), and any transfer and movements thereof. While most provisions under the Firearms Protocol refer to “firearms, parts and components and ammunition”, the marking requirements in Article 8 and in part 6 refer expressly only to firearms. In limiting the scope of application in this respect, the drafters recognized the significant extra effort that the requirement of marking every single cartouche would entail, both for manufacturers and for the public authorities designated to establish and maintain the registers. Therefore, information on parts and components and ammunition should only be kept “where appropriate and feasible” (Article 7(1) of the Firearms Protocol).

In addition, the Protocol establishes rules for confiscation, seizure and disposal of firearms, their parts and components and ammunition that represent an exception to the rules established under Articles 12–14 of the Organized Crime Convention in respect of other property used or intended for use in crime

(Article 6). While Article 6(1) regulates the confiscation of firearms, their parts and components and ammunition, and is therefore part of substantive criminal law (see below), Article 6(2) establishes provisions whereby States Parties are required to prevent illicitly manufactured and trafficked firearms from falling into the hands of unauthorized persons by seizing and destroying such firearms. In this regard, the Firearms Protocol differs significantly from the parent Organized Crime Convention. Whereas the basic policy of the Organized Crime Convention is that confiscated property should be sold for the benefit of the confiscating or other States Parties, or for the payment of compensation or restitution to victims of crime (Article 14 of the Organized Crime Convention), the inherent dangerous nature of firearms favors the policy of destruction set forth in article 6(2) of the Firearms Protocol. If States Parties wish to return seized firearms to the legal market and authorize disposal by methods other than destruction, they must ensure that those firearms have been marked and the methods of disposal have been authorized and recorded (Article 6(2) of the Firearms Protocol).

The Firearms Protocol also sets technical standards for the deactivation of firearms. If a firearm is deactivated and therefore does not come under firearms regulation any longer, it must be ensured that the deactivation is durable and irreversible (Article 9 of the Firearms Protocol). Finally, as a "must-consider" provision, Article 15 of the Firearms Protocol requires States Parties to consider measures to regulate the activities of brokers. In this regard the Arms Trade Treaty goes beyond the Protocol provisions, as its mandatory article 10 requires each State Party to take measures to regulate brokering taking place under its jurisdiction; such measures may include requiring brokers to register or obtain written authorization before engaging in brokering.

2.3.2 Substantive Criminal Law

At the heart of the Firearms Protocol are its criminal provisions – the only criminal offences related to firearms that are established on international level in a legally binding way – stipulated in Article 5(1). Each State Party is required to establish as criminal offences the

- "Illicit manufacturing[15] of firearms, their parts and components and ammunition;

15 Pursuant to Article 3 (d) of the Firearms Protocol "'Illicit manufacturing' shall mean the manufacturing or assembly of firearms, their parts and components or ammunition: From parts and components illicitly trafficked;

- Illicit trafficking[16] in firearms, their parts and components and ammunition;
- Falsifying or illicitly obliterating, removing or altering the marking(s) on firearms required by Article 8 of [the] Protocol."

The mere illicit possession of firearms does not establish a criminal offence under the Firearms Protocol, since this conduct lacks any international references as is required by the scope of application of the Organized Crime Convention and its supplementing protocols (Article 3(1) of the Convention).

Generally, these criminal provisions are not an end in themselves, but are rather intended to enable the enforcement of the legal framework – set forth in Articles 7–15 of the Firearms Protocol – within which legitimate manufacturing and transfer of firearms can take place. At the same time, the articles of the Firearms Protocol requiring the marking of firearms and comprehensive record-keeping, as well as the provision for the exchange of information between countries, recognize that criminal offences cannot be detected or prosecuted effectively without the appropriate evidence. They aim to ensure that States Parties are in a position to identify any intentional violation of the preventive regulatory and control framework, and to facilitate the prosecution and punishment of offenders. The tools contained in the Organized Crime Convention are also critical in this regard. In particular, the articles dealing with mutual legal assistance and extradition for the commission of offences covered by the Firearms Protocol are essential tools for law enforcement (see below).

Finally, as mentioned before, in accordance with Article 6(1) of the Firearms Protocol, States Parties must adopt measures to enable the confiscation of firearms, their parts and components and ammunition that have been illicitly manufactured or trafficked. Unlike the preventive seizure and destruction of such items, confiscation is a punishment whose underlying rationale is that offenders must be denied the fruits of their illegal conduct.

Without a licence or authorization from a competent authority of the State Party where the manufacture or assembly takes place; or

Without marking the firearms at the time of manufacture, in accordance with article 8 of this Protocol;

Licensing or authorization of the manufacture of parts and components shall be in accordance with domestic law."

16 Pursuant to Article 3 (e) of the Firearms Protocol "'Illicit trafficking' shall mean the import, export, acquisition, sale, delivery, movement or transfer of firearms, their parts and components and ammunition from or across the territory of one State Party to that of another State Party if any one of the States Parties concerned does not authorize it in accordance with the terms of [the] Protocol or if the firearms are not marked in accordance with article 8 of [the] Protocol."

It remains to be seen to what extent the criminal-justice approach under the Firearms Protocol is also responsive to new and emerging threats like the conversion and modification of firearms; the reactivation of deactivated firearms; polymer, modular and 3D-printed firearms; as well as contracting over the dark web; the use of postal and courier services and the use of drones for shipping. While most of the new and emerging modi operandi can technically fall under the main criminalization provisions regarding illicit manufacturing and illicit trafficking,[17] it is likely that these developments might make it necessary at some point to amend and reinforce the criminal offences and to introduce additional preventive provisions, for example with regard to online trafficking.

2.3.3 International Cooperation, Information Exchange and Prosecutorial Approaches

As firearms trafficking is often a transnational phenomenon, the ability to detect, investigate, prosecute and adjudicate this type of crime effectively rests on the exchange of information and international cooperation across borders. Therefore, Articles 12 and 13 of the Firearms Protocol establish a framework for cooperation that supplements the more general provisions of the Convention, as they call for the exchange of information relating specifically to firearms.

A key requirement of the Protocol is that the information gathered from the markings required to be placed on each firearm (Article 8 of the Firearms Protocol) and the information that must be provided and kept concerning manufacture and international transactions (Articles 7 and 10 of the Firearms Protocol) must be made available for the purpose of tracing firearms to determine whether they have been illicitly manufactured or trafficked and, if so, to support the investigation and prosecution of the offenders involved. In order to initiate and facilitate international investigations, Article 12(1) and (4) of the Firearms Protocol call on States Parties to exchange such information among themselves and to cooperate in the tracing of firearms. In this regard, any request based on the suspicion of the requesting State Party that the firearm "may have been illicitly manufactured or trafficked" must be promptly responded to. Furthermore, pursuant to article 13 of the Firearms Protocol, States Parties must identify a national body or a single point of contact in order

17 See report of the sixth session of the Working Group on Firearms "Responsiveness of the Firearms Protocol and national legislation to new and emerging threats relating to the illicit manufacturing of and trafficking in firearms, their parts and components and ammunition. Background paper prepared by the Secretariat", CTOC/COP/WG.6/2020/2.

to directly and effectively channel cooperation and the exchange of information between the authorities.

The provisions of the Firearms Protocol regarding international cooperation and information exchange are supplemented by the corresponding provisions in the Organized Crime Convention, which apply mutatis mutandis. The special investigative techniques established under Article 20 of the Organized Crime Convention, namely controlled delivery, electronic or other forms of surveillance and undercover operations, also apply. Pursuant to Article 27 of the Organized Crime Convention, States Parties are required to cooperate closely with one another to enhance the effectiveness of law enforcement action. In concrete terms, according to Article 19 of the Organized Crime Convention States Parties are encouraged to enter into agreements to conduct joint investigations, prosecutions and proceedings in more than one State in order to effectively address the transnational nature of the types of crime specified in the Organized Crime Convention and its supplementing Protocols. Also, in the context of crime with a transnational dimension, national authorities increasingly need the assistance of other States in order to successfully investigate, prosecute and punish offenders. In accordance with Article 18 of the Organized Crime Convention, all States Parties must ensure the widest measure of mutual legal assistance in investigations, prosecutions and judicial proceedings in relation to offences falling within the scope of the Firearms Protocol.

Finally, the ease of travel from country to country provides offenders with a way of escaping prosecution and justice. As extradition proceedings will then be required to bring them to justice in the prosecuting State, Article 16 of the Organized Crime Convention establishes legally binding rules with regard to such proceedings.

3 Addressing Threats at the Programme Level – A Multipronged Approach

Challenges in the implementation of the Firearms Protocol mainly arise on two different levels: the transposition of the international framework into national legislation and the enforcement of this legislation.

The exploitation of legal loopholes between countries allows criminals and terrorists to acquire firearms under better conditions with the lowest risk of detection. Only the legal harmonization of national frameworks governing firearms through the transposition of international instruments into domestic legislation will make it possible to establish common definitions, criteria and rules that enable States to cooperate more effectively and coherently when dealing with firearms trafficking and its nexus with organized crime and terrorism. Legal access to certain types and amounts of firearms and ammunition can be regulated through the enhancement of domestic frameworks by fully implementing the above-mentioned international and regional instruments.[18]

While there are usually no insurmountable obstacles to the implementation of the existing strong international and regional frameworks related to firearms through national legislation, States Parties often face fundamental difficulties in enforcing such legal frameworks. The challenges encountered by States Parties range from legal loopholes in their own or in neighboring countries to porous borders and insufficient border controls, to the lack of firearms-registries and weak institutions.

However, from a criminal justice perspective, UNODC has identified the failure to inquire into the illicit origin of seized firearms as one of the core challenges. Unless firearms are seized directly at borders or when being illicitly trafficked, it is very difficult to obtain investigative leads enabling the authorities to initiate a firearm trafficking investigation that goes beyond or in parallel to the immediate charges of illicit possession. According to the UNODC Global Study in Firearms Trafficking 2020, most illicit firearms are recovered in criminal contexts other than illicit firearms trafficking and are seized predominantly on grounds of illicit possession offences.[19]

As a rule, regardless of whether an illicit firearm is found at the crime scene of a homicide, detected in the trunk of a car at a border crossing or incidentally found during a security check on persons, law enforcement authorities will seize the firearm and initiate investigations against the holder of the firearm on the basis of the apparent criminal offence – be it homicide, illicit trafficking or simply illicit possession. However, simply seizing an illicit firearm does not interrupt the illicit arms flow. Far too often investigators focus on the primary crime instead of following the illicit firearms flow back to its source. If the investigations get stuck in this early stage, the illicit arms flow will continue unobstructed and the confiscation of the seized firearms might even create demand that can be satisfied by the very same source.

In order to durably drain the flow of illicit firearms, investigators must proactively initiate intelligence-led investigations to identify the source of the

18 See Simonetta Grassi and Spyridoula Metallinou, *The nexus between SALW, organised crime, and terrorism* (Wilton Park 2019).

19 Global Study on Firearms Trafficking – 2020.

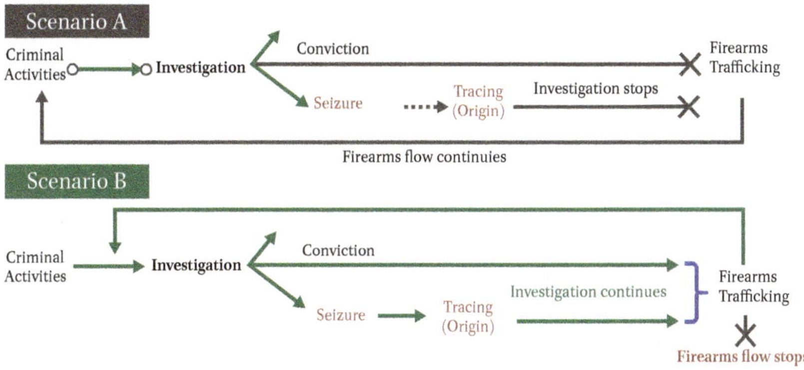

FIGURE 3 Two investigative scenarios

firearms flow. As firearms trafficking often constitutes a transnational crime extending to various jurisdictions, this may entail international cooperation among law enforcement authorities and prosecutorial services, an international exchange of information, intelligence and tracing requests channeled through national single point of contacts, and the establishment of inter-institutional or cross-regional joint investigative teams or the posting of liaison officers. The efforts of various actors combatting illicit firearms trafficking must be coordinated not only at the international level, but also at the domestic level.

When it comes to technical investigative approaches, the use of ballistic and forensic analysis as well as tracing requests can in some cases link firearms to previous crimes or to their previous owner, something that is particularly important in relation to organized crime or terrorist investigations. Also, special investigation techniques like controlled delivery, electronic or other forms of surveillance and undercover operations, as described in the UNTOC, can be useful in dealing with sophisticated organized criminal groups because of the dangers and difficulties inherent in gaining access to their operations and gathering information and evidence. In many cases, less intrusive methods will simply not prove effective, or cannot be carried out without unacceptable risks to those involved.

3.1 *UNODC's Work to Support the Implementation of the Firearms Protocol*

In 2011, in order to improve the implementation of the Firearms Protocol, UNODC launched its Global Firearms Programme – a technical assistance programme aimed at aiding Member States in preventing and countering the

FIGURE 4 UNODC Global Firearms Programme's integrated approach

problems of illicit manufacturing and trafficking in firearms, and addressing their links to other crimes, in particular organized crime and terrorism.

The programme is the first of its kind in UNODC and promotes a new paradigm, moving away from a single crime approach by looking at firearms in the broader context of transnational organized crime and terrorism and building on synergies between the international instruments in these areas.

This integrated approach rests on five interconnected pillars. Each represents specific interrelated areas of action needed to address the different aspects of the problem. None of these pillars on its own is sufficient to prevent and counter illicit arms flows, while the joint interaction of all pillars together can provide a framework for successful action and achievement of the arms component of SDG target 16.4.

The approach combines legislative assistance and the development of legal frameworks with technical support and capacity building. As part of this work, UNODC has developed several legal and technical tools to support Member States in the transposition and implementation of the Protocol, including a

Legislative Guide,[20] a Model Law[21] and a Technical Guide to implementing the Protocol,[22] as well as other analytical and technical tools.[23] Furthermore, in order to integrate preventive and security measures and support the implementation of the technical requirements established under the Protocol, in particular in the field of marking and record keeping and the collection, management and disposal of firearms. UNODC also provides law enforcement and customs agencies and prosecutors with a series of specialized training courses on the detection, investigation and prosecution of firearms trafficking and related crimes, and promotes the regular exchange of good practices and lessons learned among practitioners in this field, with a view to strengthening criminal justice responses and favoring a paradigm shift in current investigative and prosecutorial approaches. To this end, it promotes international cooperation and an exchange of information through its "Community of Practitioners" and through the sharing of case-based good practices, including through its Digest of Organized Crime Cases[24] and its forthcoming second edition focusing specifically on firearms trafficking offences. Last but not least, with a view to monitoring illicit trafficking flows and promoting stronger evidence-based policies, UNODC has launched a global annual data collection and analysis initiative to support a better understanding of the dimension, trends and patterns of firearms trafficking, and the achievement of SDG 16.4 as well as the measurement of indicator 16.4.2, which focuses on seized and traced firearms and their criminal context.[25]

---

20 Legislative Guide for the Implementation of the United Nations Convention against Transnational Organized Crime and its Protocols Thereto (https://www.unodc.org/pdf/crime/legislative_guides/05%20Legislative%20guide_Firearms%20Protocol.pdf).

21 Model Law against the Illicit Manufacturing of and Trafficking in Firearms, Their Parts and Components and Ammunition 2nd edition, 2011 (https://www.unodc.org/documents/firearms-protocol/14-08330_Firearms_revised ebook.pdf).

22 Technical Guide to the Implementation of the Protocol against the Illicit Manufacturing of and Trafficking in Firearms, their parts and components and ammunition, supplementing the United Nations Convention against Transnational Organized Crime, 2011 (https://www.unodc.org/documents/firearms-protocol/Publications/10-56148_Ebook.pdf).

23 See generally https://www.unodc.org/unodc/en/firearms-protocol/publications.html.

24 Digest of Organized Crime Cases. A compilation of good practices and lessons learned, 2012 (available in English, French, Spanish and Italian) About the initiative: https://www.unodc.org/unodc/en/organized-crime/digest-of-organized-crime-cases.html. (English text: https://www.unodc.org/documents/organized-crime/EnglishDigest_Final301012_30102012.pdf).

25 Global Study on Firearms Trafficking – 2020.

The Programme is currently active in Africa, Latin America and the Caribbean, Central Asia, Eastern Europe (Ukraine) and the Western Balkans.[26]

4 Conclusion

Nowadays, 119 States are Party to the Firearms Protocol. The parent Organized Crime Convention, by contrast, has 190 States Parties, the Protocol to Prevent, Suppress and Punish Trafficking in Persons 178 and the Protocol against the Smuggling of Migrants 150. That is why Antonio Maria Costa, former Executive Director of UNODC, used to call the Firearms Protocol the "Orphan-Protocol". The lower ratification rate remains a challenge and an incentive at the same time as the transnational phenomenon of firearms trafficking is facilitated by the exploitation of loopholes between the legal frameworks of different countries.

In the implementation process, States must take into account all regional and international instruments in this area in order to comprehensively and harmoniously address criminal justice responses as well as risk-mitigating trade regulation at the same time. Only a broadly harmonized legal framework will enable the international community to jointly address the threat of illicit firearms, related organized crime and terrorism on peaceful societies.

But even with a broadly harmonized legal framework in place, the complex – often transborder – investigation of the sources of illicit firearms – globally acting gun runners – remains a fundamental challenge. This challenge can only be addressed by comprehensive and integrated investigatory approaches that are not satisfied with short-term successes in investigations but focus on the broader picture.

States Parties to the Organized Crime Convention and the supplementing protocols thereto, have adopted a Review Mechanism in October 2018. This unique instrument will allow States Parties to the Firearms Protocol to jointly analyse the progress of implementation in an intergovernmental process. The review should not be understood as a blaming and shaming; it aims rather to "[i]mprove the capacity of States parties to prevent and combat transnational organized crime and to promote and review the implementation of the Convention and the Protocols thereto"; "help States parties to identify and substantiate specific needs for technical assistance and to promote and facilitate

26 For more details on the work of the Global Firearms Programme see https://www.unodc.org/unodc/en/firearms-protocol/index.html.

the provision of technical assistance upon their request"; and to "gather information on national legislation, successes, good practices and challenges of States parties in implementing and using the Convention and the Protocols thereto, and to promote and facilitate the exchange of this information". We remain confident that the mechanism will contribute to a better understanding of the Protocol provisions and contribute to the exchange of good practices and experiences among parties in the implementation of this important instrument.

Human Trafficking and Corruption of Public Officials

Reflections on the Interaction of the United Nations Legal Frameworks against Trafficking and Corruption

*Rosana Garciandia**

Abstract

Most countries in the world have adopted legislation tackling human trafficking and are allocating resources to fighting it. However, the content of such domestic legislation differs from country to country and its enforcement remains a challenge in many cases. In this fragmented landscape, one of the challenges in the enforcement of anti-trafficking legislation is the corruption of anti-trafficking law enforcement authorities. This article focuses on the connection between corruption and human trafficking, and on the intersection between the UN legal frameworks against human trafficking and corruption on this specific issue. The article proceeds in two parts: part 1 presents the factual connection between trafficking and corruption; part 2 analyses the intersection between the two legal frameworks and identifies some areas where there is potential for enhanced coordination.

Keywords

human trafficking – corruption – UNTOC – synergy – coordination

Introduction

Most countries in the world have adopted legislation tackling human trafficking and are allocating resources to fighting it.[1] However, the content of such

* Lecturer in Public International Law at King's College London and Research Fellow at the British Institute of International and Comparative Law

1 97 per cent of countries have enacted penal provisions addressing human trafficking (Katarina Schwarz and Jean Allain, Antislavery in Domestic Legislation Database https://

DOI:10.1163/9789004469051_007

domestic legislation differs from country to country and its enforcement remains a challenge in many cases.[2] According to the UN Office on Drugs and Crime (UNODC), 168 countries have legislation in place that criminalizes trafficking in line with the Palermo Protocol against Human Trafficking,[3] and 20 additional countries base their legislation against trafficking on definitions different from those in the Protocol. In addition, some countries have not criminalized internal trafficking, in the wrong understanding that it is not covered by the Palermo Protocol.[4]

In this fragmented landscape, in which international conventions such as the United Nations Convention against Transnational Organized Crime (UNTOC) are particularly relevant in the advancement towards convergence of national standards,[5] many challenges remain for the enforcement of anti-trafficking legislation, including those related to the transnational nature of the crime,[6] the challenges of identifying and protecting victims, and the difficulties in moving from investigation into prosecution and conviction.[7]

---

antislaverylaw.ac.uk/. By 2018, 93 per cent of the 173 States parties to the Palermo Protocol on Human Trafficking, which focuses on human trafficking and considers forced labor, sexual exploitation, slavery or servitude as forms of exploitation that the trafficking may intend to impose, had implemented legislation criminalizing sex and labor trafficking, an additional 5 per cent had implemented partial legislation and only 2 per cent had no specific trafficking offence in their domestic legislation (Sasha Jesperson and Rosana Garciandia, "Law enforcement", Delta 8.7 Thematic Overview, 2018, https://delta87.org/resources/thematic-overviews/law-enforcement/, last accessed 31 December 2020).

2 Ibid.

3 Protocol to Prevent, Suppress and Punish Trafficking in Persons Especially Women and Children, supplementing the United Nations Convention against Transnational Organized Crime (UNTOC), adopted by General Assembly resolution 55/25 of 15 November 2000, 175 States parties, in force since December 2003 ("the Palermo Protocol" or "the Protocol").

4 UNODC, *Global Report on Trafficking in Persons* (Vienna: United Nations Office on Drugs and Crime, 2018).

5 The work of certain regional systems such as the Council of Europe and the European Union has contributed to the convergence of national standards. The 2005 Council of Europe Convention on Action against Trafficking in Human Beings implemented the definition of human trafficking of the Palermo Protocol. In 2011, the European Union Directive on preventing and combating trafficking in human beings and protecting its victims took the same approach. It established minimum rules for the definition of criminal offences and sanctions on human trafficking to be adopted by EU Member States and extended the definitions and requirements of the Palermo Protocol. Belgium, Spain, France, Cyprus and the UK have modified their legislation to include, for example, explicit references to forced labor, slavery, servitude or the exploitation of criminal activities as forms of exploitation, in compliance with the Directive (S. Jesperson and R. Garciandia, "Law enforcement").

6 As the crime may occur in multiple locations and involve cross-border elements, a national response remains insufficient.

7 S. Jesperson and R. Garciandia, "Law enforcement".

One of those challenges is the corruption of anti-trafficking law enforcement authorities. Corrupt officials may turn a blind eye to trafficking networks or alert them to imminent investigations, thereby allowing them to change their tactics and compromising investigations and prosecutions. This connection between corruption and human trafficking has been noted in regional and international legislation and is the focus of this article, which presents reflections on the intersection between the UN legal frameworks against human trafficking and corruption on this specific issue. The article proceeds in two parts: part 1 presents the factual connection between trafficking and corruption; part 2 analyses the intersection between the two legal frameworks and identifies some areas where there is potential for enhanced coordination.

1 The Link between Human Trafficking and Corruption

As the UN Human Rights Council has acknowledged, there is an "increasing awareness in the international community of the detrimental impact of widespread corruption on human rights".[8] The inclusion of corruption in the UN Agenda 2030 through targets 16.4 and 16.5 confirms the relevance it has recently gained in the international arena.[9]

This awareness has extended to the trafficking and exploitation of human beings. It is widely accepted that corruption is one of the drivers facilitating the functioning of human trafficking networks and the commission of trafficking offences: corrupt border officials may facilitate the trafficking, they may be involved in the trafficking directly, and corrupt behaviors may contribute to a poor enforcement of anti-trafficking legislation.

A common case is the complicity of border guards or immigration officials who facilitate human trafficking. Bribes to immigration officials by labor recruiters may facilitate the flow of labor trafficking across borders, as has been reported about the Indo-Bangladesh border, where law enforcement agencies issue tokens to traffickers, allowing them to cross the border avoiding controls.[10]

---

8 UN Human Rights Council, Resolution 7/11, "The role of good governance in the promotion and protection of human rights", 27 March 2008.

9 Target 16.4 calls upon States to "significantly reduce illicit financial and arms flows, strengthen the recovery and return of stolen assets and combat all forms of organized crime". Target 16.5 calls upon them to "substantially reduce corruption and bribery in all their forms".

10 IBA, "Human Trafficking and Public Corruption. A Report by the IBA's Presidential Task Force Against Human Trafficking" (2016), available at https://www.ibanet.org/

In other cases, public officials are directly involved in the trafficking actions. That has allegedly been the case of Eritrean officials involved in human trafficking, according to evidence collected by the UN monitoring Group reporting on the UN Security Council's sanctions against Eritrea. It has been reported that agents of the Eritrean government trafficked people to Sudan, Israel and Egypt, after being paid sums of money previously extorted from victims.[11] The involvement of Thai public officials in the smuggling and exploitation of migrants in the national fishing industry is another outrageous example of this type of involvement.[12]

The involvement in trafficking does not only relate to state-level public officials. Public officials from diverse territorial levels or structures have reportedly been involved in trafficking on both a local and national scale. For example, in the last decade local officials in China were involved in the trafficking of persons to kilns, where they were subjected to conditions amounting to slavery.[13]

Corruption can also result in the re-trafficking of victims, as public officials may contribute to the mistreatment, misidentification or lack of protection of victims, who may end up being subject to trafficking again.[14] Even the mere appearance of corruption can facilitate the strategy of traffickers, who may dress up as members of the police, abuse their victims and discourage them from standing up for their rights.[15]

Document/Default.aspx?DocumentUid=E34FFA1D-8038-4AEC-A631-E0E2A7E0AD86, last accessed 31 December 2020, 25–26. See also Anne Peters, "Corruption as a Violation of International Human Rights", *European Journal of International Law*, Volume 29, Issue 4, November 2018, 1251–1287, on the idea of corruption as a violation of international human rights law.

11 UN, *Report of the Monitoring Group on Somalia and Eritrea pursuant to Security Council resolution 2060 (2012): Eritrea*, UN Doc S/2013/440 (2013), Annex, paras. 137–144, UN, *Report of the Monitoring Group on Somalia and Eritrea pursuant to Security Council resolution 2002 (2011)*, UN Doc S/2012/545 (2002), paras. 77–86.

12 ILO, EU, *Ship to Shore Rights: Baseline research findings on fishers and seafood workers in Thailand* (2018); ILO, *Report of the Committee set up to examine the representation alleging non-observance by Thailand of the Forced Labour Convention, 1930 (No 29), made under Article 24 of the ILO Constitution by the International Trade Union Confederation (ITUC) and the International Transport Workers' Federation (ITF)* (2017) *(GB.326/INS/16/6) (GB.329/INS/20/6)*, 14–15.

13 Ivan Franceschini (ed.), *Cronache dalle fornaci cinesi* [Chronicles from the Chinese Kilns] (Venice: Cafoscarina, 2009).

14 IBA, "Human Trafficking", 38.

15 OSCE, *Analysing the Business Model of Trafficking in Human Beings to Better Prevent the Crime* (Organization for Security and Co-operation in Europe, 2010), https://www.osce.org/secretariat/69028, last accessed 31 December 2020, 54.

Given that the corruption of public officials can be instrumental to the functioning of human trafficking networks, in order to fulfil their obligation to tackle human trafficking effectively, States need to ensure that the necessary legal provisions are in place to prevent, identify, prosecute and punish corrupt behavior of public officials at the national, regional and local levels of administration. This can be done through domestic legislation and policy, often adopted following international commitments such as the Council of Europe Convention on Action against Trafficking in Human Beings.

The mere existence of those provisions, which may consider the corruption of public officials an aggravating circumstance of a specific trafficking offence, does not however ensure an effective anti-corruption strategy as an instrument against trafficking. In Mauritania, for example, under the 2015 Anti-Slavery Act prison sentences and fines are to be imposed on law enforcement officials or the prosecutor's office when they fail to follow up on serious allegations of slavery. Persistent concerns of official complicity and corruption in slavery cases have also been reported. However, there has been no prosecution or conviction of government officials complicit in, or accused of, corruption related to human trafficking or slavery offences.[16]

States must therefore adopt the necessary legislative but also policy measures to ensure that the corruption of public officials facilitating or engaging in the trafficking of human beings is identified, tackled and sanctioned. It must be noted that, in accordance with the International Law Commission Articles on Internationally Wrongful Acts of States (ARSIWA), the acts or omissions of a public official constituting a violation of an international obligation are attributable to the State, even if those public officials are acting *ultra vires*.[17]

2 The Palermo Protocol against Trafficking and Its Connection to the UN Convention against Corruption (UNCAC): Synergies and Opportunities for Further Coordination

The intersection between trafficking and corruption raises interesting questions on the actual connection between the UN legal frameworks tackling corruption (UNCAC) and organized crime (UNTOC). Although the link between

16 United States Department of State, 2019 TIP Report.

17 Philippa Webb and Rosana Garciandia, 'State Responsibility for Modern Slavery: Uncovering and Bridging the Gap', *International and Comparative Law Journal*, vol 68, July 2019, 539–571.

trafficking and corruption is generally accepted, the two frameworks seem to continue working in silos to some extent. This can be explained by the different scope of the two UN conventions, with the UNCAC focusing on corruption, understood as a wide concept[18] including bribery, embezzlement, trading in influence, abuse of functions, and illicit enrichment,[19] and the UNTOC focusing on transnational organized crime. Nevertheless, given how instrumental corruption can be to transnational organized crime and with both instruments being administered by the UN Office on Drugs and Crime (UNODC), a higher level of coordination between the two frameworks seems desirable.

This need has been confirmed by the UNODC, which is tasked with implementing both conventions, as it has called on States parties to the UNTOC to take into account the obligations under the UNCAC when implementing the UNTOC.[20] In addition, several UNODC initiatives have recently explored the link between trafficking and corruption. An illustrative example is a workshop that UNODC organized in 2018, where sub-region, civil society and government experts from Cambodia, Myanmar, Thailand and the Lao PDR came together to map out the links between corruption and human trafficking and to brainstorm concrete steps for tackling the problem; corruption and a lack of accountability were identified as factors underpinning migration-related crime across the region.[21]

Looking at the legal provisions of the UNTOC on trafficking, there is no cross-reference between the Palermo Trafficking in Persons Protocol and the UNCAC, and indeed no reference in the former to corruption at all. Article 10 of the Palermo Protocol covers obligations of law enforcement, immigration and other relevant authorities but is limited to creating obligations for States to cooperate by exchanging information. Under this provision, States parties are called upon to provide or strengthen training for the officials involved, and the obligation to share information that may enable other authorities to detect victims and traffickers. From the perspective of the connection between

18 Mark Pieth, "What is corruption?", in Fritz Heimann and Mark Pieth, *Confronting Corruption* (Oxford: OUP, 2018), 32.

19 Cecily Rose, *International Anti-Corruption Norms: Their Creation and Influence on Domestic Legal Systems*, Introduction (Oxford Scholarship Online, October 2015).

20 UNODC, Legislative Guides for the Implementation of the United Nations Convention against Transnational Organized Crime and the Protocols Thereto (United Nations, 2004) 81–82, 84 available at www.unodc.org/pdf/crime/legislative_guides/Legislative%20 guides_Full%20version.pdf, last accessed 31 December 2020.

21 https://www.unodc.org/southeastasiaandpacific/en/laopdr/2018/04/corruption-human -trafficking/story.html, last accessed 31 December 2020.

trafficking and corruption, the content of this provision may be seen as a lost opportunity for a cross-reference, compared to the model adopted by the European Union or the Council of Europe.

Under Article 4.3 of EU Directive 2011/36/EU on preventing and combating trafficking in human beings and protecting its victims, the fact that a trafficking offence is committed by public officials in the performance of their duties is regarded as an aggravating circumstance.[22] Likewise, under article 24 of the Council of Europe Convention on Action against Trafficking in Human Beings, the fact that the offence was committed by a public official in the performance of his/her duties must be considered by States Parties as an aggravating circumstance in their domestic legal framework.[23]

In comparison with the approach adopted by the Council of Europe and the EU, the lack of such a provision in the Palermo Protocol on Trafficking could suggest a weaker legal framework against corruption in connection to trafficking. It should be noted, however, that the UNTOC and UNCAC frameworks establish core minimum obligations, and nothing prevents States parties to the Palermo Protocol from adopting a stronger approach. In fact, EU Member States or States parties to the Council of Europe Convention which are also parties to the Palermo Protocol are under such an obligation as parties to these two frameworks. For example, in 2014 Cyprus adopted Law 60(I)/2014 on Prevention and Combating of Trafficking and Exploitation of Persons and the Protection of Victims, whereby the commission of trafficking by a public official in the performance of his/her duties is considered as an aggravating circumstance.[24]

While including such a provision in the Palermo Protocol could be a positive development, the difficulties of reaching an agreement on this point must be considered, and therefore other forms of cooperation become relevant as a means for overcoming the challenge of such a reform.[25] One of the alternative

22 Directive 2011/36/EU of the European Parliament and of the Council of 5 April 2011 on preventing and combating trafficking in human beings and protecting its victims, and replacing Council Framework Decision 2002/629/JHA.

23 Council of Europe Convention on Action against Trafficking in Human Beings, adopted by the Committee of Ministers of the Council of Europe on 3 May 2005.

24 Group of Experts on Action against Trafficking in Human Beings (GRETA), 5th General Report on GRETA's Activities, covering the period from 1 October 2014 to 31 December 2015, 14.

25 To understand the complexities of the international legal framework in this area, see Pierre Hauck and Sven Peterke, eds. *International Law and Transnational Organised Crime* (Oxford: OUP, 2016); Margaret E. Beare, ed. *Critical Reflections on Transnational Organized Crime, Money Laundering and Corruption* (Toronto: University of Toronto Press, 2003); United Nations, Travaux préparatoires of the negotiations for the elaboration of the

ways to enhance cooperation is to rely on the work of the Conferences of the States Parties and UNODC in the process of implementation of the two conventions. The UNCAC implementation review mechanism, administered by the UNODC, is a positive example of how, despite States having chosen to create anti-corruption norms with a non-binding content,[26] States can work together towards more protective domestic systems against corruption. States parties to the two conventions submit their reports for analysis by the Conference of the States Parties within their respective mechanisms for reviewing the implementation of the conventions.[27] Given the cumbersome reporting process and the limited resources States have, they may use parts of one report to fulfil their reporting obligations on different but related conventions. This fact could be used as an opportunity to encourage States to think strategically about their work in tackling the way in which corruption may be hampering their fight against human trafficking, even if no provision of the Palermo Protocol asks them to do so. States receive technical assistance and recommendations from UNODC and the Conference of the States Parties. That assistance could encourage a more comprehensive understanding of the two conventions.

Other relevant institutions in the areas of corruption and transnational organized crime have also called for such enhanced coordination. The International Bar Association, for example, has suggested joint task forces with the participation of anti-corruption and anti-trafficking experts, integrated anti-corruption and human trafficking legislation, and a more fluent dialogue between the two areas.[28] The same approach has been recommended at the Council of Europe level by the Group of Experts on Action against Trafficking in Human Beings (GRETA), which has called for higher levels of coordination with the Group of States against Corruption (GRECO), the Council of Europe's own anti-corruption body.[29]

United Nations Convention against Transnational Organized Crime and the protocols thereto (United Nations Office on Drugs and Crime, 2006).

26 On the limitations of the UNCAC, see C. Rose, *International*, Introduction, 10.

27 The mechanism for the review of the implementation of the UNTOC and its protocols was established only in 2018. See Conference of the Parties to the United Nations Convention against Transnational Organized Crime, Establishment of the Mechanism for the Review of the Implementation of the United Nations Convention against Transnational Organized Crime and the Protocols thereto, 19 October 2018, CTOC/COP/2018/L.4/Rev.1.

28 IBA, "Human Trafficking", 52.

29 Group of Experts on Action against Trafficking in Human Beings (GRETA), *3rd General Report on GRETA's Activities, covering the period from 1 August 2012 to 31 July 2013* (Strasbourg: Council of Europe), 24.

3 Conclusions

The role of public officials in the fight against a complex transnational crime such as human trafficking is crucial, as they are entrusted by the State with the task of enforcing anti-trafficking legislation, identifying victims, preventing the action of trafficking networks and investigating the crimes committed in their territory. The link of public officials to the State does not only make their role relevant. It also can engage the responsibility of the State if its international obligations are breached by the corrupt behavior of a public official.[30]

States must therefore put in place the necessary legislative and policy measures to ensure that no act or omission of their public officials facilitates or contributes in any way to the trafficking of human beings. States may do this on their own initiative, but international and regional legal frameworks are also highly influential in advancing towards a higher convergence of standards. This could be achieved through provisions that define the corruption of public officials as an aggravating circumstance in the case of a trafficking offence, as envisaged in the EU and Council of Europe frameworks.

The UN legal frameworks on corruption (UNCAC) and trafficking (UNTOC and Palermo Protocol) do not contain a provision of this kind and, although there is an increasing appetite for higher levels of coordination, the two conventions continue to be applied in an independent way. The reporting obligations that the two conventions create could present an interesting opportunity to encourage States to coordinate their efforts against trafficking and corruption, despite such a clause not being part of the Palermo Protocol. Technical assistance by UNODC and the sharing of promising practices may encourage States to follow that model and contribute to a more integrated response.

30 Under Article 4 of the ILC Articles on the Responsibility of States for Internationally Wrongful Acts, the "conduct of any State organ shall be considered an act of that State under international law, whether the organ exercises legislative, executive, judicial or any other functions, whatever position it holds in the organization of the State, and whatever its character as an organ of the central Government or of a territorial unit of the State".

The Obligations of Prevention, Protection and Assistance to Victims of Trafficking

*Ruth Shrimpling and Annelies Blondé**

Abstract

The emphasis on the prevention of the crime and the protection and assistance to victims of crime in international and European anti-trafficking instruments is a prominent example of the human rights-based approach to human trafficking. However, there is room for further improvement. This article reflects on the needs of trafficking victims in light of theoretical and practical implications of relevant international and European instruments with the aim of defining future action.

Keywords

trafficking victims – human rights – Victim Support Europe

Introduction

Trafficking in human beings is nowadays very much regarded as a human rights violation, which follows *inter alia* from the explicit prohibition of trafficking in Article 5 of the Charter of Fundamental Rights of the European Union.[1] The emphasis on the prevention of the crime and the protection and assistance to

* Victim Support Europe. This article is written following a presentation delivered by Victim Support Europe (VSE) during a conference on the implementation of the Palermo Convention, titled "The Obligations of Prevention, Protection and Assistance to Victims of Crime". In representing the voices of victims and victim support services across Europe and beyond, Victim Support Europe has 30 years of experience in advocating for the rights of victims of all crime. In doing so, particular focus is paid to giving a voice to the most vulnerable victims, such as victims of trafficking in human beings.

1 European Union, Charter of Fundamental Rights of the European Union, OJ C 326, 26.10.2012, 391–407, Article 5.

 | DOI:10.1163/9789004469051_008

victims of crime in international and European anti-trafficking instruments is a clear example of this human-rights based approach. However, there is room for further improvement. This article reflects on the needs of trafficking victims in light of theoretical and practical implications of relevant international and European instruments with the aim of defining future action.

1 The Needs of Victims

Five key needs can be distinguished for all victims of crime: the need for respect and recognition, the need for support and information, the need for access to justice, the need for protection and the need for compensation and restoration. In order for any justice system to effectively comply with its obligations towards victims of crime, it should meet all those needs. Apart from their common general needs, victims of crime have specific needs linked to specific groups, such as victims of terrorism or victims of human trafficking, and linked to their individual needs.

Vulnerability is a common feature among victims of human trafficking.[2] This vulnerability renders the victims more susceptible to further exploitation by traffickers.[3] As a result, trafficking victims may be distrustful of authorities and institutions, and highly traumatised – to the extent that their views do often not correspond to reality.[4]

Apart from having suffered psychological trauma and physical injuries, they may fear retaliation or repercussions towards themselves or their family members.[5] In addition, their situation is often exacerbated by their migration status, having been trafficked as undocumented migrants or depending on precarious, short-term visas or other permits. Also due to a lack of resources or legal means to return safely to their home countries, or circumstances in their home countries which forced them to leave, victims are stranded without recourse to another viable option, under the control of their traffickers.[6] Thus, trafficking victims as a group require firewalls for safe reporting and have heightened protection needs.

2 Human Rights Monitoring Institute, *Communicating with Victims of Crime: a Handbook for Officers*, (HRMI, 2018), 39–40, available at: https://victimsupport.eu/activeapp/wp-content/files_mf/1554799348HandbookforOfficersHRMI2.pdf, last accessed 31 December 2020.

3 Ibid.

4 Ibid.

5 Group of Experts on Action against Trafficking in Human Beings ("GRETA"), *8th General Report on GRETA's Activities*, (Strasbourg, Council of Europe 2018), 37, available at: https://rm.coe.int/8th-/168094b073, last accessed 31 December 2020.

6 Ibid.

It should be noted that more than half of registered trafficking victims in the European Union are trafficked for the purposes of sexual exploitation, according to data collected in EU member states from 2015–2016.[7] Statistics show that an overwhelming majority of registered victims trafficked for these purposes are female.[8] Statistically speaking alone, the crime of trafficking clearly has a gendered dimension. This gendered dimension should be taken into account in the provision of protection and assistance measures for victims of trafficking. For instance, most victims require immediate access to healthcare and mental health services, in order not only to address sexual health and reproductive needs, but also to begin treatment for the many traumas they will have been subjected to.[9]

2 VSE and the Needs of Victims of Crime

VSE is an umbrella organisation comprising of over 60 members worldwide, comprised of national victim support services, NGOs, State actors, academia, Law Enforcement Agencies, policy makers, governmental institutions and individuals. Established in 1990, VSE promotes the rights and services to all victims of crime across Europe and beyond through advocating to improve EU and international laws, through research and knowledge development, and through capacity building at a national and regional level. VSE membership covers 31 countries, and spans from Canada, across Europe, to New Zealand – with many regions in between. VSE and its member organizations represent the victims' voice, as well as the voice of victim support organisations across the globe.

Our work is grounded on the firm belief that the obligations enshrined in international, European and national legal instruments should be implemented effectively in practice, with a victim-centred perspective. In advocating for the needs of all victims of crime, VSE develops and contributes to projects across Europe and beyond. For instance, VSE recently finalised the VOCIARE project, which assessed the practical implementation of the Directive 2012/29/EU of the European Parliament and of the Council of 25 October 2012 establishing

---

7 European Commission, *Data Collection on Trafficking in Human Beings in the EU*, (Brussels, European Union, 2018), 55, available at: https://ec.europa.eu/home-affairs/sites/homeaffairs/files/what-we-do/policies/european-agenda-security/20181204_data-collection-study.pdf, last accessed 31 December 2020.

8 Ibid., 18.

9 Heather J. Clawson and Nicole Dutch, *Addressing The Needs Of Victims Of Human Trafficking: Challenges, Barriers, And Promising Practices*, (United States, US Department of Health and Human Services, 2008), 2.

minimum standards on the rights, support and protection of victims of crime, and replacing Council Framework Decision 2001/220/JHA (Victim's Directive) in the EU.[10] Having analysed legislation and policies in 26 EU Member States and surveyed almost 800 victim support professionals in Europe, research findings granted a comprehensive understanding of the functioning and the failures of the Victims' Directive.[11] Based on this research, the VOCIARE Synthesis Report identifies key gaps and develops clear recommendations for EU wide action.[12]

Over the years, VSE has also developed constructive working relationships with EU institutions. Amongst others, VSE significantly contributed to the Report "Strengthening victims' rights: from compensation to reparation", published by Ms Joëlle Milquet in March 2019 in her role as Special Adviser to former European Commission President, Jean-Claude Juncker. This Report calls for a shift from a needs-based towards a human rights-based approach as well as a shift towards reparation, thereby allowing for non-pecuniary forms of reparation to be awarded.[13]

Whilst VSE advocates and promotes the rights and services for all victims of crime, we also recognise the additional lengths necessary to protect society's most vulnerable victims. Victims of trafficking should – in theory – be able to exercise the rights and protective measures guaranteed under the EU Victims' Rights Directive, although – as we will see in the coming paragraphs – this may not always ring true in reality. Moreover, due to the extraordinary level of vulnerability within this victim group, various European and international legal instruments add to existing rights in an aim to address the many shortcomings and bottlenecks trafficking victims face.

3 Legal and Policy Framework

Both under international and European law, trafficking in human beings is explicitly prohibited and regarded as a criminal enterprise and a serious human rights violation. The Protocol to Prevent, Suppress and Punish Trafficking in Persons, Especially Women and Children, supplementing the

10 Victim Support Europe and APAV, *Victims of Crime Implementation Analysis of Rights in Europe Synthesis Report ("VOCIARE Synthesis Report")*, (VSE, 2018), 14–15. Read online via: https://victimsupport.eu/activeapp/wp-content/files_mf/1564677465VOCIARE_Synthesis_Reportweb.pdf, last accessed 31 December 2020.

11 Ibid.

12 Ibid.

13 Joëlle Milquet, *Strengthening victims' rights: from compensation to reparation*, (Brussels, European Commission, 2019), 33–34.

United Nations Convention against Transnational Organized Crime (the 'Palermo Protocol'),[14] is the oldest and most widely used legal source in the international anti-trafficking framework.[15] This Protocol, which was adopted by UN General Assembly Resolution A/RES/55/25 on 15 November 2000, has been ratified by 175 Parties, including the EU.[16] Its aim was to harmonise international legislation on the topic of trafficking in persons and to stress the need for a human rights-based approach towards trafficking victims.[17] In 2004, UN Office of the High Commissioner for Human Rights established the position of Special Rapporteur on trafficking in persons, especially women and children.[18]

The Council of Europe Convention on Action against Trafficking in Human Beings of 16 May 2005 (the 'Council of Europe Anti-Trafficking Convention')[19] is the main regional human rights treaty in Europe dealing with the phenomenon of trafficking in human beings in a comprehensive manner. This Convention has been signed and ratified by all CoE Member States, except for Russia, and is open to non-CoE members.[20] The text of the Convention adopts a holistic, human rights-based approach to combatting trafficking and thereby focuses

14 United Nations General Assembly, *Protocol to Prevent, Suppress and Punish Trafficking in Persons, Especially Women and Children, supplementing the United Nations Convention against Transnational Organized Crime, UNGA resolution* 55/25, 15 November 2000.

15 European Institute for Gender Equality, *Gender-specific measures in anti-trafficking actions*, (EIGE, 2018), 21, available at: https://ec.europa.eu/anti-trafficking/sites/antitrafficking/files/read_the_report_gender-specific_measures_in_anti-trafficking_actions.pdf, last accessed 31 December 2020.

16 Council of the European Union, *Decision of 24 July 2006 on the conclusion, on behalf of the European Community, of the Protocol to Prevent, Suppress and Punish Trafficking in Persons, Especially Women And Children, supplementing the United Nations Convention Against Transnational Organised Crime concerning the provisions of the Protocol, in so far as the provisions of this Protocol fall within the scope of Articles 179 and 181a of the Treaty establishing the European Community, OJ L* 262, 22.09.2006, 44–50; Council of the European Union, *Decision of 24 July 2006 on the conclusion, on behalf of the European Community, of the Protocol to Prevent, Suppress and Punish Trafficking in Persons, Especially Women And Children, supplementing the United Nations Convention Against Transnational Organised Crime concerning the provisions of the Protocol, in so far as the provisions of the Protocol fall within the scope of Part III, Title IV of the Treaty establishing the European Community, OJ L* 262, 22.9.2006, 51–58; Denise Charlton and Associates, *Protecting Victims: An Analysis of the Anti-Trafficking Directive from the Perspective of a Victim of Gender-Based Violence*, (EIGE, 2017), 21.

17 Denise Charlton and Associates, *Protecting Victims: An Analysis of the Anti-Trafficking Directive from the Perspective of a Victim of Gender-Based Violence*, 22.

18 UN OHCHR, 21/04/2004, Special Rapporteur on trafficking in persons, especially in women and children, *UN Doc.* E/CN.4/DEC/2004/110.

19 Council of Europe, *Convention on Action against Trafficking in Human Beings and its Explanatory Report ("Council of Europe Anti-Trafficking Convention")* (Warsaw, 16.v.2005), *Council of Europe Treaty Series* 197, Article 4(a).

20 GRETA, *8th General Report on GRETA's Activities*, 73–74.

on the "three P's" prevention, protection and prosecution.[21] The Convention clearly sets out the importance of early identification mechanisms and the need for a multidisciplinary approach.[22] Additionally, the Convention establishes an independent monitoring mechanism, namely the Group of experts on action against trafficking in human beings (GRETA), tasked with evaluating the implementation of the Convention by State Parties.[23]

In recent years, the EU has established a broad legal and policy framework concerning the topic of trafficking in human beings. In its 2012–2016 Strategy on the Eradication of Trafficking in Human Beings, trafficking was identified as a complex transnational phenomenon with specific vulnerabilities, such as having gender-based violence and social inequalities as important root causes.[24] This EU Strategy identified a number of key priorities, including the prevention, protection and assistance of trafficking victims, and actions to be completed by EU institutions and EU member states within a certain timeframe in combatting this phenomenon.[25] In light of these priorities, the Commission produced a document in 2013 setting out a detailed overview of the rights of victims of trafficking under EU legislation, referring to the applicable EU Directives, some of which will be discussed below, and the Charter of Fundamental Rights of the European Union.[26]

While abovementioned policy documents are an important monitoring tool and showcase the EU's prioritisation of the phenomenon, they are *in itself* not legally binding, unlike the relevant EU legislation. The core of the EU's legislative package is the Directive 2012/29/EU of the European Parliament and of the Council of 25 October 2012 establishing minimum standards on the rights,

---

21 Secretariat of the Committee on Equal Opportunities for Women and Men Parliamentary Assembly of the Council of Europe, *Handbook for parliamentarians The Council of Europe Convention on Action against Trafficking in Human Beings* (Strasbourg, Council of Europe, 2007), 15–16, available at: http://lastradainternational.org/lsidocs/637%20Trafficking-human-beings_E.pdf, last accessed 31 December 2020.

22 *Council of Europe Anti-Trafficking Convention*, Article 10; Conny Rijken and Alice Bosma, *A review of the implementation of the EU strategy on human trafficking by EU members*, (TRACE, 2014), 19, available at: https://pure.uvt.nl/ws/portalfiles/portal/5078137/TRACE_D1.1_A_review_of_the_implementation_of_the_EU_strategy_on_Human_trafficking_by_EU_members.pdf, last accessed 31 December 2020.

23 *Council of Europe Anti-Trafficking Convention*, Article 36; GRETA, *First General Report on GRETA's Activities*, (Strasbourg, Council of Europe, 2011), 9–11, available at: https://rm.coe.int/greta-2011-11-genrpt-en/16807b4d71, last accessed 31 December 2020.

24 European Commission, *The EU Strategy towards the Eradication of Trafficking in Human Beings 2012–2016*, COM/2012/0286, 2–3.

25 Ibid., 6–8 (priority A and B) and 16–18.

26 European Commission, *The EU rights of victims of trafficking in human beings* (Brussels, European Union, 2013), https://ec.europa.eu/anti-trafficking/sites/antitrafficking/files/eu_rights_of_victims_of_trafficking_en_1.pdf, last accessed 31 December 2020.

support and protection of victims of crime, and replacing Council Framework Decision 2001/220/JHA, commonly referred to as the Victims' Directive.[27] The Victims' Directive lays down a number of rights applicable to all victims of crime in the EU, regardless of their residence status.[28] Under this Directive, victims have the right to understand and be understood, the right to information, the right to support, the right to participate in criminal proceedings, the right to protection and individual assessment amongst others, whilst also including the rights of the victims' family members. Article 22 of Victims' Directive, the text of article 22 of the Victims' Directive explicitly refers to trafficking victims in connection with the right to an individual assessment.[29]

The specific needs of victims of trafficking are further addressed in Directive 2011/36/EU of the European Parliament and of the Council of 5 April 2011 on preventing and combating trafficking in human beings and protecting its victims, and replacing Council Framework Decision 2002/629/JHA, hereafter referred to as the Anti-Trafficking Directive.[30] The Anti-Trafficking Directive defines the crime of trafficking in the same manner as the Palermo Protocol and the Council of Europe Anti-Trafficking Convention, thereby ensuring legal certainty and a common understanding of this phenomenon.[31] This definition moreover reflects the three constitutive elements of trafficking in human beings: the 'act', the 'method' or the 'means' and the 'purpose' or the 'aim'.[32] The 'act' refers to the way in which a person is trafficked or moved. This action can include for instance the sale, purchase or the recruitment of the person as well as the act of holding the person captive.[33] The 'means' or 'methods' are the different mentally or physically abusive mechanisms used to gain control of the person and to affect their will, such as the use of force, fraud and coercion.[34] The 'aim' of trafficking is the exploitation of the person for the purposes of

27 VSE and APAV, *VOCIARE Synthesis Report*, 14.

28 European Parliament and Council of European Union, *Directive 2012/29/EU of 25 October 2012 establishing minimum standards on the rights, support and protection of victims of crime, and replacing Council Framework Decision 2001/220/JHA ("Victims' Directive")*, *OJ L* 315, 14.11.2012, 57–73.

29 Ibid., Article 22.

30 European Parliament and Council of European Union, *Directive 2011/36/EU of 5 April 2011 on preventing and combating trafficking in human beings and protecting its victims, and replacing Council Framework Decision 2002/629/JHA ("Anti-Trafficking Directive")*, *OJ L* 101, 15.04.2011, 1–11.

31 Denise Charlton and Associates, *Protecting Victims: An Analysis of the Anti Trafficking Directive from the Perspective of a Victim of Gender-Based Violence*, 25.

32 Ibid.

33 Ibid.; Human Rights Monitoring Institute, *Communicating with Victims of Crime: a Handbook for Officers*, 39.

34 Ibid.

slavery or forced labour, the performance of sexual services or prostitution, forced marriage, organ harvesting, etc.[35] Like the Council of Europe Anti-Trafficking Convention, the Anti-Trafficking Directive aims at providing a comprehensive, human rights-based approach to combat trafficking in line with the explicit prohibition thereof in Article 5 of the Charter of Fundamental Rights of the European Union.[36] In doing so, this Directive focuses on the prevention of trafficking, the protection of its victims and the prosecution of offenders, to each of which it ties specific State obligations.[37] In light of its holistic approach, this Directive also links the provisions of victims' assistance to EU legislation in the field of migration, in particular the Directive 2004/81/EC on the residence permit issued to third-country nationals who are victims of trafficking that allows for EU Member States to grant temporary residence permits throughout the length of judicial proceedings.[38]

4 Theory vs. Reality

Despite the broad international and European legal framework on trafficking, the law is not always fully implemented nor applied in practice. For the purposes of this article, focus will be laid on the implementation of the obligations of prevention, protection and assistance of trafficking victims in Europe.

With regard to assistance, states should ensure that at least a number of generic and specialist support services are unconditionally accessible to all victims of crime based on the text of the Victims' Directive.[39] These services should be accessible to victims and their family members, making services accessible to those in remote rural communities as well as in metropolitan, urban areas. Even more pressing than the need for greater accessibility of services, is the existence of the services themeselves. Legislative requirements on every EU Member State to provide a generic, national victim support service are still not respected by some countries.[40]

Furthermore, victims' access to support services is often hindered by additional access conditions. In some Member States, trafficking victims are for instance required to report the crime to the police before getting access to

35 Ibid.

36 *Charter of Fundamental Rights of the European Union*, Article 5; *Anti-Trafficking Directive*, recital 7.

37 Conny Rijken and Alice Bosma, *A review of the implementation of the EU strategy on human trafficking by EU members*, 17–18.

38 *Anti-Trafficking Directive*, recital 17.

39 VSE and APAV, *VOCIARE Synthesis Report*, 60–61.

40 Ibid.

support services, and in the majority of EU States, reporting a crime as an undocumented victim of crime implies a major risk of arrestation, detention and eventual deportation.[41]

In cross border situations, trafficking victims are further excluded from accessing national support services both in the country where the crime was committed, given the requirement of residence status, as well as in their country of residence, given the lack of effective referral systems.[42] In an effective referral system, a number of individuals, agencies and organisations work together closely and exchange information and communication in a quick manner with the aim of catering for the particular needs of every victim.[43] Victims can make initial contact with any of the service providers connected to the network, following which they will benefit from all services offered by the network depending on their specific needs.[44] In reality, no such comprehensive referral systems exist and trafficking victims are usually referred to the same organisations or shelters despite their varying individual needs.

With regard to protection, both the Victims' Directive and the Anti-Trafficking Directive call for an individual assessment of victims to identify their specific protection needs.[45] Individual protection measures should prevent instances of secondary and repeat victimisation. The majority of EU Member States, however, fails to establish systematic procedures.[46] As a result, such assessment is conducted on a case-by-case basis or with the use of questionnaires.[47] Given that trafficking victims have heightened protection needs, the lack of a structured process and targeted approach is particularly worrying.

With regard to prevention, the European Commission discussed the scope of some preventative measures in more detail in its second progress report on the fight against trafficking. It held that awareness-raising campaigns and trainings should target the impact of trafficking rather than the demand of services delivered by trafficking victims.[48] It further called upon all EU

---

41 Victim Support Europe, *A Journey from Crime to Compensation: An analysis of victims' access to compensation in the EU*, (VSE, 2019), 35.

42 Ibid.

43 Asian Development Bank, *The Significance of Referral System as a Response to Human Trafficking and Unsafe Migration*, (ADB, 2009), 3 en 25–26, available at: http://lastradainternational.org/lsidocs/human-trafficking.pdf.

44 Ibid.

45 *Anti-Trafficking Directive*, Article 12; *Victims' Directive*, Article 22.

46 VSE and APAV, *VOCIARE Synthesis Report*, 156–157.

47 Ibid.

48 European Commission, *Second report on the progress made in the fight against trafficking in human beings (2018) as required under Article 20 of Directive 2011/36/EU on preventing and combating trafficking in human beings and protecting its victims*, COM/2018/0777, 6–8.

Member States to criminalise the actions of those who knowingly make use of services provided by trafficking victims, including businesses.[49] In light of trafficking, the aim of training should be towards raising awareness amongst frontline professionals on the particular needs of trafficking victims in order to reduce instances of secondary victimisation, and to encourage early detection of victims.[50]

Police officers may commonly be the first people to communicate with trafficking victims, as such they should be adequately trained in victim-oriented communication, and needs-assessments in order to assess the victims' most urgent needs.[51] However, EU Member States generally fail to provide mandatory, comprehensive training modules on victims' rights and victims' needs for judges, prosecutors, police officers and social workers.[52]

The lack of adequate and practical implementation of the three abovementioned obligations towards trafficking victims significantly hampers their access to justice as well as their access to compensation and restoration. Trafficking victims refrain from reporting the crime out of fear of inappropriate treatment of police officers, reprisals at the hands of their traffickers, both of which are largely enabled by the lack of safe and anonymous reporting mechanisms.[53]

Even where the crime has been reported and criminal proceedings against the offender have been instigated, excessive length of the proceedings poses a disproportionate burden on trafficking victims.[54] In a case concerning trafficking in human beings, the European Court for Human Rights has recently held that authorities need to act with haste especially in cases where vulnerable victims are to be removed from harmful situations.[55] Regarding access to compensation, budgetary constraints restrict recourses to compensation to certain types of violence and certain forms of damage, thereby effectively excluding non-physically violent crimes such as trafficking.[56] Where they are not prevented from claiming compensation, trafficking victims must seek compensation from the offender first.[57] Given the level of control that was exercised by

---

49 Ibid.

50 Human Rights Monitoring Institute, *Communicating with Victims of Crime: a Handbook for Officers*, 41.

51 Ibid., 42.

52 VSE and APAV, *VOCIARE Synthesis Report*, 167.

53 VSE, *A Journey from Crime to Compensation: An analysis of victims' access to compensation in the EU*, 86.

54 Ibid., 51–52.

55 ECtHR, *L.E. v Greece, Appl. No.* 71545/12, 21 January 2016, § 82–85 and 97–98.

56 VSE, *A Journey from Crime to Compensation: An analysis of victims' access to compensation in the EU*, 42–43.

57 Ibid., 44.

the offender over the trafficked victim, the requirement to seek compensation from the offender can provoke the feeling of being controlled by them all over again and, thus, significantly increase the risk of revictimisation whilst maintaining unwanted and traumatic contact with the offender.[58]

5 Conclusion

Despite the comprehensive legal and policy framework at a European level, trafficking victims are too often prevented from gaining access to various support services in practice. This is mainly caused by States' failure to properly implement the obligations of prevention, protection and assistance towards victims enumerated in the relevant legal instruments. In order to improve the actual situation of trafficking victims in Europe, a victim-centred approach addressing the gaps identified in this article should be developed in practice. These services should be fully accessible to victims of crime, including their family members, in an unconditional manner, regardless of the type of crime and the individual circumstances of the victim. Member States should further set up comprehensive referral mechanisms between generic and specialist victim support services, thereby ensuring that each victim receives assistance according to their specific needs, and systematic mechanisms for individual assessment, thereby limiting revictimisation and ensuring an individual approach to individual situations. Trafficked victims should have access to reporting firewalls, safe and anonymous reporting mechanisms which allow them to report trafficking without repercussion on their residency status, and with no communication between law enforcement and immigration authorities relating to the residency status of the reporting victim. Given their particular vulnerability, trafficked victims have heightened protection needs and require additional safeguards. Failure to properly address the needs of trafficking victims hinders their access to justice and to compensation, thus hindering their road to recovery whilst dissuading other trafficked victims to come forward through the belief that no positive actions will be taken. A full and unfettered access to a wide range of victim support services paves the way to restorative justice processes for trafficked victims.

58 Ibid.

The Smuggling Protocol and the Criminalization of Humanitarian Activities at Sea

*Laura Salvadego**

Abstract

This paper focuses on some recent events of criminalization of humanitarian activities at sea in Italy, and precisely the *Open Arms* and the *Sea Watch 3* cases. It is stated that criminalization of humanitarian activities at sea is largely due to a substantial 'implementation gap' between the Smuggling Protocol and the current EU legal framework on people smuggling, that is the so-called 'Facilitators' Package' of 2002. It is further contended that legal certainty requirements make legislative reform necessary in Italy to prevent the criminalization of humanitarian activities at sea.

Keywords

Smuggling Protocol – crime of facilitating illegal immigration – Open Arms – Sea Watch 3

Introduction

Since their adoption, the concrete implementation of the United Nations Convention against Transnational Organized Crime (UNTOC)[1] and its Additional Protocols on human trafficking and migrants smuggling[2] within

---

* Associate Professor of International Law at the University of Macerata, Department of Political Science, Communication and International Relations.

1 United Nations Convention against Transnational Organized Crime (UNTOC), adopted by the UN General Assembly in New York on November 15, 2000 with Resolution No. 55/25 (2000), in force since 29 September 2003, *UNTS* vol. 2225, 209.

2 Cf. Protocol against Smuggling of Migrants by Land, Sea and Air annexed to the Convention (Smuggling Protocol), adopted by the UN General Assembly on 15 November 2000 with Resolution No. 55/25 (2000), *UNTS* vol. 2241, 507, in force since 28 January 2004. Protocol

 | DOI:10.1163/9789004469051_009

the domestic legislation of the States Parties has brought to light some loopholes and shortcomings. An interesting aspect to be highlighted as regards the implementation of the Smuggling Protocol[3] in recent experience is the high level of criminalization of humanitarian activities at sea both in Europe and in Italy. This seems to be largely due to a substantial 'implementation gap' between the Smuggling Protocol and the European Union (EU) legal framework on people smuggling.

1 The Implementation Gap at the EU Level

Current EU legislation in the area is represented by the so-called 'Facilitators' Package' of 2002. It is composed of the Council Directive No. 2002/90 of 28 November 2002, defining the facilitation of unauthorized entry, transit and residence and the Council Framework Decision No. 2002/946, implementing that directive.[4] This legislation, however, is not fully consistent with the Smuggling Protocol as regards how it deals with those providing humanitarian assistance to irregular migrants.[5] Indeed, the Facilitators' Package omits to provide that in order for the facilitation of irregular entry into a Member State to be considered a crime there must be an economic gain, a criminal intent and a link to an organized transborder organization.[6]

Inconsistencies between the EU legal framework and the Smuggling Protocol with respect to the criminalization of humanitarian activities at sea can be found in relation to two main aspects: i) the definition of 'economic

to Prevent, Suppress and Punish Trafficking in Persons, Especially Women and Children, supplementing the Convention (Trafficking Protocol), adopted by the UN General Assembly on 15 November 2000 with Resolution No. 55/25 (2000), *UNTS* vol. 2237, 319, in force since 25 December 2003.

3 On this issue, see the analysis by Alessandro Spena, above.

4 European Commission, "Refit Evaluation of the EU Legal Framework against Facilitation of Unauthorized Entry, Transit and Residence: The Facilitators Package Directive 2002/90/EC and Framework Decision 2002/946/JHA," Doc. SWD(2017) 117.

5 In this regard, see also Sara Bellezza and Tiziana Calandrino, "Criminalization of Flight and Escape Aid. Borderline Europe," March 2017, https://www.borderline-europe.de/sites/default/files/readingtips/Kidem%20final%20report%2005_2017.pdf (last accessed February 2, 2021); Charles Heller and Lorenzo Pezzani, "Blaming the Rescuers," Forensic Oceanography, 2017, www.blamingtherescuers.org/report/ (last accessed February 2, 2021).

6 In this regard, see e.g. Sergio Carrera *et al.*, "Fit for Purpose? The Facilitation Directive and the Criminalisation of Humanitarian Assistance to Irregular Migrants," *European Parliament Study*, 2016, Doc. PE 536.490, https://www.europarl.europa.eu/RegData/etudes/STUD/2016/536490/IPOL_STU(2016)536490_EN.pdf (last accessed 2 February 2021).

gain' in the description of the 'facilitation of irregular entry' and ii) the inclusion of an exemption from punishment for those providing humanitarian assistance.

As regards the first element, Article 3(a) of the Smuggling Protocol defines the smuggling of migrants as "the procurement, in order to obtain, directly or indirectly, a financial or other material benefit, of the illegal entry of a person into a State Party of which the person is not a national or a permanent resident". Furthermore, Article 6(1)(a) of the Smuggling Protocol specifically requires "a financial or other material benefit" as a condition for the criminalization of procuring irregular entry. This aspect, however, is not included in the EU legal framework concerning migrant smuggling. In fact, Article 1(1)(a) of the Facilitation Directive does not consider financial gain as being strictly necessary in order to criminalize the facilitation of irregular entry. According to Article 1(1)(a), indeed, "[e]ach Member State shall adopt appropriate sanctions on: any person who intentionally assists a person who is not a national of a Member State to enter, or transit across, the territory of a Member State in breach of the laws of the State concerned on the entry or transit of aliens".

With respect to the second aspect, on the other hand, the preparatory works for the Smuggling Protocol make clear that the reference, in the definition of smuggling of migrants, to both 'criminal intent' and 'the financial or other material benefit' as elements of the offence is intended to exclude from punishment "the activities of those who provide support to migrants for humanitarian reasons, including non-governmental organizations".[7] Article 1(2) of the Facilitation Directive, by contrast, only provides a non-binding option to EU Member States to apply an exception to the criminalization of facilitation of irregular entry when it is humanitarian in nature. According to Article 1(2): "[a]ny Member State may decide not to impose sanctions with regard to the behaviour defined in paragraph 1(a) by applying its national law and practice for cases where the aim of the behaviour is to provide humanitarian assistance to the person concerned." This means that the implementation of the 'humanitarian assistance exception' is limited and based on a discretionary will of the EU Member States.

As a result, EU national legislations show a number of 'grey areas' and non-governmental organizations (NGOs) are often deterred from providing

7 See UNODC, "Model Law against the Smuggling of Migrants," 27 October 2010, referring to the Interpretative notes, A/55/383/Add.1, para. 88, and *Travaux Préparatoires*, 469; cf. Daniel Ghezelbash *et al.*, "Securitization of Search and Rescue at Sea: The Response to Boat Migration in the Mediterranean and Offshore Australia," *International and Comparative Law Quarterly* 67 (2018), 347–348: 322.

assistance because of the concrete risk of being subject to criminal prosecution in the State involved. Such a situation has arisen precisely after the intervention of NGOs in the Central Mediterranean Sea to carry out SAR activities – for which the coastal States are responsible, but which they do not always perform – mainly from 2016 onwards after the so-called 'migrant crisis' due to the non-international armed conflict in Libya. The action of NGOs, in fact, has been perceived as creating a 'magnet effect' or 'pull factor', which serves both to encourage and facilitate the deeds of human traffickers and migrant smugglers.[8] In particular, Frontex has maintained that smugglers are able to adapt their routes on the basis of where SAR operations take place.[9] Furthermore, the joint communication adopted by the European Commission and the High Representative for Foreign Affairs and Security Policy in regard to the management of migrant flows and the safeguarding of lives in the Central Mediterranean focused attention on NGO SAR activities with reference to their operating area or the activities carried out near the Libyan coasts.[10]

The concern was raised that rescue activities in the maritime areas closest to Libya were likely to change traffickers' *modus operandi*, inducing them to embark migrants on dinghies completely unsuitable for navigation and with which there was no possibility of being able to reach the European coasts, as they could count on relief efforts near the Libyan territorial sea or even inside it;[11] such activities would thus effectively facilitate the business of smugglers and traffickers.[12] These suspicions have since translated into a number of charges against NGOs in several EU Member States.

In the EU action plan against migrant smuggling for the years 2015–2020, the European Commission announced proposals to improve both Council

8 For a demonstration of the baselessness of this assertion, see Elias Steinhilper and Rob Gruijters, "Border Deaths in the Mediterranean: What We Can Learn from the Latest Data," *Border Criminologies Blog*, 8 March 2017.

9 See Frontex, "Risk Analysis for 2016," March 2016, www.frontex.europa.eu/assets/Publications/Risk_Analysis/Annula_Risk_Analysis_2016.pdf, 39 (last accessed February 2, 2021).

10 European Commission and High Representative of the Union for Foreign Affairs and Security Policy, Joint Communication to the European Parliament, the European Council and the Council, "Migration on the Central Mediterranean Route Managing Flows, Saving Lives," Brussels, 25 January 2017, Doc. JOIN(2017) 4 final, 6.

11 Ibid., 6.

12 Frontex Agency Director, interview with the German newspaper Die Welt: Manuel Bewarder and Lisa Walter, "Rettungseinsätze vor Libyen müssen auf den Prufstand," *Die Welt*, 27 February 2017, www.welt.de/politik/deutschland/article162394787/Rettungseinsaetze-vor-Libyen-muessen-auf-den-Pruefstand.html (last accessed 2 February 2021).

Directive No. 2002/90 and Council Framework Decision No. 2002/946. In particular, the objective was precisely to strengthen the criminal framework aimed at combating the facilitation of illegal entry and residence, while avoiding the risk of criminalizing people who provide humanitarian assistance to migrants in distress.[13] To date, however, no changes to this effect have been introduced into European legislation.

2 The Case of Italy

As regards Italian legislation, the crime of facilitating illegal immigration is established under Article 12(1) of Legislative Decree No. 286/1998, which regards the conduct of promoting, directing, organizing, financing or carrying out the transportation of foreigners into the territory of the State or carrying out other acts aimed at illegally procuring entry into the territory of the State. Here the element of 'financial gain' is considered just as an aggravating circumstance and not such as a constitutive element of the crime.

Article 12(2) specifically provides for a 'humanitarian assistance exception', stating that the relief and humanitarian assistance provided in Italy to foreigners who are present in the territory of the State and are in need of assistance do not constitute a crime. This, however, has not prevented the activists of NGOs from being targeted. In fact, the 'humanitarian exception' only explicitly considers humanitarian activities provided in Italy to foreigners who are in need of assistance and are already present in Italy. The exception does not seem to be applicable to humanitarian activities on the high seas, where search and rescue (SAR) activities usually take place.[14] The provision also explicitly refers to the exemption established by Article 54 of the Italian Criminal Code as regards the 'state of necessity'. The Italian Court of Cassation has often invoked Article 54(3) for the specific purpose of sanctioning smugglers for their illicit acts entirely committed on the high seas and to exempt rescuers from liability (and punishment) for acts partially committed within Italian jurisdiction and

13 European Commission, Communication from the Commission to the European Parliament, the Council, the European Economic and Social Committee and the Committee of the Regions, EU Action Plan against migrant smuggling (2015–2020), COM(2015) 285 final, 27 May 2015, 4, https://eur-lex.europa.eu/legal-content/EN/TXT/?uri=celex%3A52015DC0285 (last accessed 3 February 2021).

14 In this regard see also Silvia Bernardi, "I (possibili) profili penalistici delle attività di ricerca e soccorso in mare," *Diritto penale contemporaneo* (2018): 134–144: 143. *Contra* Paolo Morozzo della Rocca, *Immigrazione, asilo e cittadinanza: discipline e orientamenti giurisprudenziali* (Rimini: Maggioli, 2016), 290.

leading to the disembarkation of migrants in Italy.[15] However, legal commentators have highlighted that this reasoning does not seem to be legally well grounded.[16] The conduct of rescuers is rather exempted from liability under Article 51 of the Italian Criminal Code, which establishes an exemption for 'fulfilment of duties'. Their conduct, in fact, is fully consistent with the duty "to render assistance to any person found at sea in danger of being lost", codified under Article 98 of the United Nations Convention on the Law of the Sea (UNCLOS).[17]

In Italy, in explicit reference to the allegations launched by Frontex,[18] several investigations were opened into the alleged 'collusion' between NGOs and Libyan traffickers.[19] Following investigations carried out by a Sicilian Public Prosecutor's Office, the suspicion spread that some NGOs active along the Central Mediterranean route were responsible for encouraging irregular immigration to Italy or even providing help to those responsible for migrant smuggling and human trafficking. In several instances, the master and crew of a vessel that had saved people at sea and successively disembarked them in an Italian harbor were charged with violating Italian domestic laws on the prohibition of illegal migration or even with other offences.[20]

15 Cf. e.g. Court of Cassation, Criminal section I, Judgment of 27 March 2014, No. 14510/2014. See also Court of Cassation, Criminal section I, Judgment of 22 December 2015, No. 11165/2016, *Cassazione penale* (2016), 3847.

16 See Alessandra Annoni, "Il ruolo delle operazioni Triton e Sophia nella repressione della tratta di esseri umani e del traffico di migranti nel Mediterraneo centrale," *Il diritto dell'Unione europea* (2017): 829–860 at 853–854.

17 On this duty see Irini Papanicolopulu, "The Duty to Rescue at Sea, in Peacetime and in War: A General Overview," *International Review of the Red Cross* 98 (2016), 491–514: 503.

18 Cf. Alessandra Ziniti, "Migranti, sulle Ong Zuccaro insiste: Notizie date da Frontex, non ho nuove prove," *la Repubblica*, 3 May 2017, available at: www.repubblica.it/cronaca/2017/05/03/news/ong_migranti_scafisti_procura_catania_zuccaro-164500643/ (last accessed February 2, 2021). *Supra*, para. 1.

19 These concerns had clearly emerged in the remarks presented to the Senate Defense Committee by the Director of Frontex and the Prosecutor in Chief of Catania: cf. Italian Senate Defense Committee, Document approved by the fourth permanent Commission at the conclusion of the fact-finding survey on the contribution of Italian soldiers to the control of migratory flows in the Mediterranean and the impact of the activities of non-governmental organizations, 16 May 2017, Doc. XVII No. 9, www.senato.it/japp/bgt/showdoc/frame.jsp?tipodoc=SommComm&leg=17&id=01022634&part=doc_dc-sedetit_pi-genbl_icscdmiacdfmnmeli&parse=no (last accessed 2 February 2021).

20 Thus, for instance, some members of the NGO *Médecins sans Frontières* were investigated for alleged illegal disposal of a large quantity of dangerous waste posing an infectious risk; the waste was claimed to have been dumped by the *Aquarius* and *Vos Prudence* vessels between January 2017 and May 2018. However, this line of inquiry as well proved to be devoid of any foundation.

Thus, the judgments issued in the cases *Open Arms*[21] and *Sea Watch 3* must be welcome. In their judgments the Italian Courts clarified the substance of the crime of facilitating illegal immigration under Article 12 of the Legislative Decree No. 286/1998 and the basis on which criminal charges must be excluded in relation to the captain of the ship and the staff of NGOs involved in SAR activities at sea.

The *Open Arms*, a rescue ship belonging to the NGO Proactiva Open Arms, was impounded by the Italian authorities on March 27, 2018[22] and later released on April 16, 2018.[23] The captain of the ship and some other members of the crew belonging to the Spanish NGO were investigated for criminal association[24] and aiding irregular immigration.[25]

On March 15, 2018, the Italian Rescue Coordination Centre (RCC) informed the *Open Arms* of the presence of a dinghy travelling on international waters off the Libyan coast. The *Open Arms* was heading towards it when the Libyan Coast Guard took over the coordination of the SAR operations and ordered the NGO vessel to stay out of sight.[26] However, when it arrived near the scene of the incident, the *Open Arms* did not see the Libyan Coast Guard vessel and decided to proceed with the rescue operations. It then sailed towards a second dinghy that had been spotted in the meantime; while embarking people from this second boat, the Libyan Coast Guard arrived and ordered the NGO vessel not to approach the migrants. The *Open Arms* crew, after ascertaining the inaction of the Libyan Coast Guard, still managed to complete the rescue of the people from the second dinghy and headed north, in search of a 'place of safety' where it could disembark the migrants. A third inflatable boat was instead intercepted by the Libyans and the migrants who occupied it were disembarked in Libya. The *Open Arms* reached the Italian coast and was authorized to disembark the rescued people in Pozzallo, in Sicily. Shortly after the

---

21 Tribunal of Ragusa, Order of confirmation of the decree of the pre-trial judge, 11 May 2018.

22 Tribunal of Catania, Decree of validation and preventive seizure, 27 March 2018, 11 https://www.statewatch.org/media/documents/news/2018/apr/it-open-arms-sequestration-judicial-order-tribunale-catania.pdf (last accessed 3 February 2021).

23 Tribunal of Ragusa, Decree rejecting a request for preventive seizure, 16 April 2018, https://newsmagnify.it/wp-content/uploads/2018/08/Decreto-di-rigetto-di-richiesta-di-sequestro-preventivo-GIP-di-Ragusa-16-Aprile-2018.pdf and Tribunal of Ragusa, Order to confirm the decree of the pre-trial judge, 11 May 2018, https://www.dirittoimmigrazionecittadinanza.it/allegati/fascicolo-n-2-2018/254-trib-ragusa-11-52018 (both last accessed 3 February 2021).

24 Article 416 Italian Criminal Code.

25 Article 12 Legislative Decree No. 286/1998.

26 Tribunal of Ragusa, Decree rejecting a request for preventive seizure, 16 April 2018, 3.

safe landing, the NGO was informed that the Catania Prosecutor had issued an order to impound the vessel and charged some members of the crew with belonging to a criminal organization and smuggling migrants.[27]

The order for the pre-trial seizure of the *Open Arms* vessel focused on whether it was plausible to assume that the defendants had committed a crime. In particular, the judge examined whether the conduct of the *Open Arms* crew, which had refused to hand over the migrants to the Libyan authorities and had brought them to Italy, should be considered migrant smuggling. For its own part, the NGO argued that the crew had acted out of necessity, citing Article 54 of the Italian Criminal Code in their defense: the unlawful conduct was to be considered as justified because of the necessity to protect rescued migrants from a current danger of a serious harm. On the one hand, the pre-trial judge noted that the migrants were not in imminent danger because their dinghies, despite being overcrowded, were not leaking, the weather conditions were good and the Libyan Coast Guard was ready to intervene. On the other hand, however, the judge also stated that the *Open Arms* could not be obliged to hand over the migrants to the Libyan authorities because Libya could not be considered a 'safe place' for landing.[28] As a consequence, as long as the situation remained unchanged, the refusal of the members of the NGO to hand over the migrants to the Libyan authorities and the decision to bring them to Italy was justified.

The Tribunal of Ragusa clarified that the crime of facilitating illegal immigration established under Article 12(1) of Legislative Decree No. 286/1998 is considered to have been committed only if there is the subjective element consisting in the awareness of promoting, directing, organizing, financing or carrying out illegal transportation of foreigners into the territory of the State or other acts aimed at illegally procuring entry into the territory of the State. Furthermore, no crime of facilitating illegal immigration is considered to have been committed in the absence of any agreement or collaboration with smugglers who organize departures and when constant communication is maintained with the Italian RCC during the rescue operation and the landing is made with the authorization of the Italian authorities.[29]

---

27 For a detailed description of the facts, see Francesca De Vittor, "Soccorso in mare e favoreggiamento dell'immigrazione irregolare: sequestro e dissequestro della nave Open Arms," *Diritti umani e diritto internazionale* 12 (2018)<. 443–453.

28 See again Tribunal of Ragusa, Decree rejecting a request for preventive seizure, 16 April 2018, 3.

29 Regarding this issue see also De Vittor, "Soccorso," 451–452.

The same conclusion was also reached by the Tribunal of Agrigento and the Court of Cassation in the case *Sea Watch 3*.[30] On June 26, 2019, after the vessel had rescued 53 persons in the Libyan SAR region and spent fifteen days off Lampedusa, the master of the ship, due to the critical conditions of migrants on board, decided to enter Italian territorial waters, thus violating the formal order whereby the Italian Government had forbidden the vessel to enter, transit or stop in the territorial sea of the State. On June 29, 2019, the master of the ship decided to enter the Italian harbor to disembark migrants and she was investigated for alleged resistance and violence against public officials for not having complied with the order to stop and for having hit an Italian patrol boat while docking. The judge held that the captain's conduct was legitimate in that she was acting in fulfillment of the duty to rescue persons in danger at sea. In fact, Libya could not be considered a safe place for disembarkation of migrants and the rescue operations could only be considered to have reached completion with the landing of migrants in a safe place. The judge also established that the Decree Law giving the Italian Minister of the Interior the authority to adopt formal measures limiting or prohibiting ships engaged in the disembarkation of persons in violation of Italian laws, as well as the entry, transit or stopping thereof in the territorial sea, and providing for the imposition of fines and the possibility of seizing the ship in the event of a repeated offence, was not applicable in the case of vessels engaged in SAR activities at sea because their actions could not be considered a threat to public security.[31]

Both the pre-trial order in the *Open Arms* case, later confirmed by the Tribunal, and the decisions adopted by the Tribunal of Agrigento and the Court of Cassation in the *Sea Watch 3* case are laudable.[32] In a criminal law perspective, they clarified the nature of the offence of facilitating illegal immigration under Article 12 Legislative Decree No. 286/1998 and on what basis it

30 Tribunal of Agrigento, Decision No. 2592 of July 2, 2019, http://www.altrodiritto.unifi.it/adirmigranti/rackete-ordinanza-rigetto.pdf; Court of Cassation, Decision No. 6626, February 2020, http://images.processopenaleegiustizia.it/f/sentenze/documento_Ab8Hv_ppg.pdf (both last accessed February 3, 2021).

31 Cf. Decree Law No. 53 of June 14, 2019, "Urgent provisions on public order and security," entered into force on June 19, 2019, Official Gazette No. 138, June 14, 2019, and later amended by Decree Law No. 130 of October 21, 2020, entered into force on October 22, 2020, Official Gazette No. 261, 21 October 2020.

32 For some human rights considerations see Laura Salvadego, *The Respect for Fundamental Human Rights in the Fight against Human Trafficking and Migrant Smuggling across the Central Mediterranean Sea* (Leiden/Boston: Brill, 2019): 83–84.

should be ruled out in the case of NGO staff operating in the Mediterranean.[33] First of all, liability for commission of the crime is conditional on the existence of the subjective element consisting in the awareness of promoting, directing, organizing, financing or carrying out illegal transport of foreigners into the territory of the State or performing other acts aimed at illegally procuring entry into the territory of the State. Moreover, no crime is considered to have been committed in the absence of any collaboration with smugglers who organize departures or when constant communication is maintained with the Italian RCC during the rescue operation and a landing is made with the authorization of the Italian authorities and in the place indicated by them.[34] Indeed, rescue operations only end with the landing of migrants in a safe place. Consequently, the transport of migrants to the 'place of safety' designated by the competent RCC must be considered as a part of the rescue obligation. The same still holds true even when the landing is made without the authorization of the Italian authorities, as in the case of the NGO vessel *Sea Watch 3*. This interpretation appears to be the only one compatible with applicable international obligations binding Italy, and precisely with Articles 3 and 6 of the Smuggling Protocol and the customary rule on the duty to rescue people found in danger at sea codified under Article 98 of the UNCLOS.

3 Concluding Remarks

The interpretation of the offence of facilitating illegal immigration under Article 12 Legislative Decree No. 286/1998 accepted by Italian Courts in the above-mentioned cases appears to be the only one compatible with applicable international law obligations binding Italy, specifically the Smuggling Protocol and the customary rule on the duty to rescue people found in danger at sea codified under the UNCLOS. However, legal certainty requirements make legislative reform necessary in Italy and also in other EU States to prevent the criminalization of humanitarian activities at sea.

It would be desirable, indeed, for States to amend their criminal legislation so as to make sure that no criminal charges may be levied against those who provide support to migrants for humanitarian reasons. Thus, for instance, in Italy, as seen, Article 12(2) Legislative Decree No. 286/1998, distinguishes 'aiding

33 Tribunal of Ragusa, Order of confirmation of the decree of the pre-trial judge, 11 May 2018.

34 Regarding this issue, see again De Vittor, "Soccorso," 451–452.

and abetting' from 'humanitarian assistance'.[35] The unclear formulation of the provision, however, has not prevented volunteers and activists from being prosecuted. In fact, even if charges are eventually dropped or the master and crew of the vessels of relief organizations are eventually declared innocent, bringing charges against them and impounding their vessels produce negative consequences for migrants in danger at sea as evidenced by the growing number of deaths at sea since the start of legal action against NGOs.

35 See *supra*, para. 2.

International Cooperation to Counter Migrant Smuggling and Human Trafficking through Special Investigative Techniques

Challenges in the Implementation of the International Legal Framework Regulating Undercover Operations in the Italian Legal System

*Eugenio Zaniboni**

Abstract

The adoption of international coordination measures to spread the use of 'special investigative techniques' to combat organised crime effectively is encouraged by Article 20 of the UNTOC. This article discusses, firstly, the main features of 'undercover operations' involving, or taking place in, more than one State. It then examines the Italian implementation legal framework, as amended by a new law passed in 2019, seeking to establish whether and to what extent Italy is complying with its international commitments in this field.

Keywords

special investigative techniques – Decreto sicurezza – Human Trafficking Victims Protection Act – irregular migration

Introduction

The United Nations Convention against Transnational Organised Crime (UNTOC) encourages international coordination measures to broaden the use of 'special investigative techniques' in combating multi-dimensional threats posed by organised crime effectively.[1] According to its Article 20, under the

* Ph.D., Assistant professor in International Law, University of Foggia.

1 United Nations Convention against Transnational Organized Crime (hereinafter "UNTOC" or "Palermo Convention"), 15 December 2000, in force since 29 September 2003, art. 20, para. 1.

 | DOI:10.1163/9789004469051_010

heading of "*Special investigative techniques*", each State Party is allowed to take the necessary measures to organize "[i]f permitted by the basic principles of its domestic legal system [...] and under the conditions prescribed by its domestic law [...] the use of other special investigative techniques, such as electronic or other forms of surveillance and undercover operations." The provision is aimed at "effectively combating organized crime". The meaning and the scope of the provision is not limited to operations involving only the territorial State.[2] This is clear if we look at the text of Article 20(2), which affirms that "States Parties are encouraged to conclude, when necessary, appropriate bilateral or multilateral agreements or arrangements for using such special investigative techniques in the context of cooperation at the international level."

Scholars and practitioners recognize that conducting investigations that can lead to a positive judicial outcome often entails high risk and is very expensive. Moreover, it always requires a thorough knowledge not only of international (and European) rules but also of the legal system of territorial States, as for instance, in order to accurately collect the required criminal evidence.

Judicial or independent oversight of the use of these techniques is required, together with strict observance of principles of legality, subsidiarity and proportionality. It is also well known by law enforcement operators that, as safeguards against potential abuses of authority, if the national criteria regarding the validity of collected evidence are not scrupulously met and observed, such evidence may not be employed during the trial. Consequently, cross border policing efforts are often likely to be weakened due to a lack of both detailed instruments of coordination and information among States and a clear legal and practical arrangement.[3]

See: Phil Williams and Dimitri Vlassis, *Combating Transnational Organized Crime: Concepts, Activities, and Responses*, *Transnational Organized Crime* 4, (2001), UNODC, *Legislative Guides: United Nations Convention against Transnational Organized Crime*, New York, 2004; David Mclean, *Transnational Organized Crime – A Commentary to the UN Convention and its Protocols*, Oxford, 2007; Gioacchino Polimeni, "The Notion of Organised Crime in the United Nations Convention against Transnational Organized Crime", in Stefania Carnevale, Serena Forlati and Orsetta Giolo (editors) *Redefining Organised Crime: A Challenge for the European Union?* (Oxford: Hart, 2017), 57–74.

2 On the nature and scope of States' obligations to cooperate in the investigation and prosecution of smugglers and their accomplices see Anne T. Gallagher and Fiona David, *The International Law of Migrant Smuggling* (Cambridge: Cambridge University Press, 2014).

3 This is one of the reasons why the European Union, in view of supporting, streamlining and facilitating cross-border operations and information exchange, adopted at least two detailed practical guides on the topic: *The European Manual on cross-border operations*, Brussels, 11 September 2017, 11840/17 (491 pages), and *The Manual on Law Enforcement Information Exchange*, containing all the practical information necessary for carrying out cross-border operations (116 pages). See also Conference of the Parties to the United Nations Convention

Sometimes, the inability to improve policing cooperation across borders is attributable to a deficiency of mutual trust. These difficulties are often explained by international public lawyers as an (enduring) problem of retaining sovereignty.[4] But they can undermine the main purpose of the Convention, namely, "to promote cooperation to prevent and combat transnational organized crime more effectively". This is the reason why Article 27 of the Palermo Convention is wholly dedicated to creating a framework of legal measures aimed at enhancing cooperation among Member States according to the best available techniques. In the absence of specific agreements, Article 20(3) provides that States' "decisions to use such special investigative techniques at the international level shall be made on a case-by-case basis". They should also "take into consideration financial arrangements and understandings with respect to the exercise of jurisdiction by the States Parties concerned".

The purpose of the present article is to discuss this interesting and innovative tool provided by the Convention in connection with the Italian legal framework and the evolving topic of "undercover operations". This investigation technique was improved with a bill approved in 2019. Although the new rules governing undercover operations feature several noteworthy aspects, as we will try to show here, they have not yet received any particular attention. We will discuss the issue in the following paragraphs, also with the aim of establishing whether and to what degree Italy is meeting its international commitments.

1 New Italian Rules on Undercover Operations after the Implementation of Law Decree No. 53/2019

The Italian law ratifying the Palermo Convention, which introduced this new legal tool,[5] is a relatively recent one. It is interesting to observe that Italy has shown a special interest in combating the phenomenon of smuggling since the late 1990s. It proposed to the International Maritime Organisation ('IMO') the adoption of a Convention specifically designed to combat migrant

---

against Transnational Organized Crime ('CTOC'), *Good practices in special investigative techniques*, Vienna, 7 August 2013, CTOC/COP/WG.7/2013/2.

4 Article 20(2) of UNTOC provides that appropriate bilateral or multilateral agreements or arrangements for using such techniques at the international level shall be concluded and implemented in full compliance with the principle of sovereign equality of States and shall be carried out strictly in accordance with the terms of those agreements or arrangements.

5 Article 9, Law no. 146 of 16 March 2006, in *Gazzetta Ufficiale della Repubblica Italiana*, n. 85 of 11 April 2006, available at www.parlamento.it/parlam/leggi/06146l.htm.

smuggling by sea. The purpose of this proposal was to criminalise the smuggling of migrants by sea under international law.[6] The IMO's Legislative Committee, however, felt that the proposal was primarily a matter of international criminal law that went well beyond maritime issues, and thus beyond the IMO's mandate. The Italian draft thus constituted the matrix of a specific "Protocol against the Smuggling of Migrants by Land, Sea and Air" added to the Palermo Convention.[7] Nevertheless, it took Italy about seven years to ratify the UNTOC. Law No. 146 of 2006 grants immunity, under Article 51 of the Italian Criminal Code, to a comprehensive category of undercover judicial police officers.[8] However, the law was vaguely worded and among other things did not provide for any allocation of economic resources.

One might think that the Italian legislator has been pushed to introduce "undercover police operations" as a special technique of enquiry (in principle not part of the Italian legal tradition)[9] because it was one of the requirements – or let us say formalities – Italy needed to fulfil in order to achieve accession to the Palermo Convention, rather than as a means of fighting more effectively against domestic and transnational crime networks according to recognised international best practices of conducting investigations. It may be interesting, therefore, to analyse it in the light of a recent law decree, commonly called the "*Decreto sicurezza*", which contains some specific provisions about undercover operations.[10]

---

6 IMO Legal Committee, Proposed Multilateral Convention to Combat Illegal Migration by Sea, IMO Doc LEG 76/11/1 (1 August 1997). On the topic: Andree Kirchner and Lorenzo Schiano di Pepe, "International Attempts to Conclude a Convention to Combat Illegal Migration," *International Journal of Refugee Law*, 1998, n. 4, 662–674.

7 United Nations Office on Drugs and Crime ('UNODC'), *Travaux Préparatoires of the Negotiations of the United Nations Convention against Transnational Organized Crime and the Protocols thereto* (United Nations, 2006), 451. See also Andreas Schloenhardt and Jessica Dale, "Twelve Years On: Revisiting the UN Protocol against the Smuggling of Migrants by Land, Sea and Air", *Zeitschrift für Öffentliches Recht/Journal of Public Law*, 2012, 129–156; UNODC, *Global Report on Trafficking in Persons 2020*, Vienna, 2021.

8 Some commentators have argued that these categories are too wide and indefinite. Given the delicate nature of the tasks assigned to the law enforcement officers, the legislation may not help to preserve and protect some specific features inherent in this type of activity: see, for instance, art. 9(1) and (2) of the UNTOC.

9 Even if deployment of spies and informants to gather information on rivals and subjects was described by the Romans. See Edward Gibbon, *The History of the Decline and Fall of the Roman Empire*, Vol. 1. New York, 1831, 221. A brief history of undercover operations is in Edwin W. Kruisbergen, Deborah de Jong and Edward R. Kleemans, "Undercover Policing. Assumptions and Empirical Evidence", *British Journal of Criminology*, 2011, 394–412.

10 Law decree No. 53 of 14 June 2019, *Disposizioni urgenti in materia di ordine e sicurezza pubblica*, Gazzetta Ufficiale della Repubblica Italiana, No. 138 of 14 June 2019 (hereinafter

2 The New Italian Bill and the Goal of "Strengthening Investigative Coordination in the Field of Crimes Related to Illegal Immigration": A Reached Target or a Missed Opportunity?

For the first time, the new bill allots 3 million euros over the three-year period 2019/21, to be used to "implement the use of the investigative tool of undercover operations", and, in particular – and this is the first perplexing statement, as we are going to make clear – to cover costs "resulting from the participation of law enforcement officers from States with which special agreements have been signed *for their deployment on national territory*."[11] Moreover, the budget allocation provided for in the "*Decreto sicurezza*" is classified as "urgent" and "necessary" also in view of the need "to strengthen investigative coordination in the field of crimes related to illegal immigration", and "the instruments to combat this phenomenon".[12]

Let us immediately say that, given such objectives, one would have expected an intervention of broader scope, more geared towards pursuing of the overall objectives of the Palermo Convention and such as to provide the competent Authorities with a whole range of technical instruments and trained human resources for this purpose. But the decree is surprising in this respect for several different reasons, as we will see.

Firstly, it is hard to understand why the aim and the scope of the new decree are so limited. For instance, it provides for the supply of funds and technical equipment only to foreign law enforcement officers operating in Italy and does not include the Italian agents deployed abroad. The enquiries aimed at dismantling the international networks of smugglers and traffickers who illegally bring migrants into Italy, may involve, as we noted above, the use of significant economic resources and also require specific activities abroad. Providing for the needed resources is not only an indispensable logistical and organizational prerequisite. It is a *logical consequence of the transnationality of the crimes*. In other words, in each of the States involved in the transit of migrants it is necessary to provide for the deployment of adequate means and equipment for the tasks to be carried out, as well as a sufficient number of specifically trained law enforcement operators,[13] who are able to bring to light, at the cost of prolonged

"*Decreto sicurezza*"). The converted law is No. 77 of 8 August 2019, Gazzetta Ufficiale della Repubblica Italiana, No. 186 of 9 August 2019.

11 See art. 4 of "*Decreto sicurezza*" (italics added).

12 Ibid.

13 See in this respect Article 29 of the Palermo Convention: "Each State Party shall, to the extent necessary, initiate, develop or improve specific training programmes for its law enforcement personnel."

and complex investigation activities, the techniques and complicity used to evade national controls.[14]

No one could say that the investigations conducted have been wholly accomplished insofar as it has not been possible to attribute a name and a face to each member of the criminal association, including the founders and main beneficiaries of the association's financial proceeds. This is of course a hard target to reach in every circumstance. If there is insufficient evidence to support prosecution, or it will take too long or be too costly (in terms of both finances and resources) to prosecute, disrupting a crime or criminal group is usually better than doing nothing at all.[15]

It is worth noting that smugglers have created, over time, a well-established organizational model in each of the States in which they operate. It is a well-proven operational model which can be described as having a 'horizontal' rather than 'vertical' structure and, given its nature, requires highly targeted investigative activities. The aim of these investigations is to reconstruct the route taken by the transported migrants by tracing it backwards. This is a really difficult task, since the organizations are used to acting on the basis of an organizational model that provides for a preordained segmentation of criminal conduct, whereby each member of the association has a minor role (e.g. driver or food supplier or guardian of the areas in which the migrants pass, and so on). For this reason, none of the participants is aware of what happens before or after his or her limited contribution to the planned criminal operation.

The fragmentation of activities, which take place in different States, is not only an effective method of reducing individual responsibilities. It is also a system that can provide the organizational leaders of the association with a greater guarantee of impunity since none of the individual members is able to recognise them or knows their identity. Thus, it can be easily understood why this entails a very complex type of investigation which, in order to bring about results, must take place within a framework characterized by a high level of coordination between the various enforcement and judicial authorities of the States involved, with due observance of the rules for the exercise

14 A comprehensive report of EUROPOL, *Trafficking in Human Beings, Financial Business Model*, The Hague, 2015, explains the financial aspect of the human trafficking operating model, how proceeds are laundered and where they are invested. According to the report it is difficult to estimate the overall profits derived from trafficking of human beings. In 2005, the international Labour Organization estimated that the yearly profits of this illicit activity in the world exceed EUR 29.4 billion. ILO, *Forced Labour and Human Trafficking: Estimating the Profits*, Working Paper No. 4, Geneva, 2005.

15 UNODC, *Toolkit to Combat Smuggling of Migrants. Tool 7 – Law enforcement and prosecution*, Vienna, September 2010, 14.

of national jurisdictions, as well as the procedural and substantive guarantees provided for by the respective domestic legal systems.[16]

As we noted above, however, the *Decreto sicurezza* is not concerned with strengthening the tools and resources available to Italian agents operating abroad. The scope of application of Article 4, in fact, is curiously limited to the exclusive benefit of operations that will be carried out by foreign officers hosted on Italian territory. This limitation conferred on the provision seems even more surprising in the light of the fact that at the time the *Decreto sicurezza* was approved, the Italian Government had just been 'downgraded' in the US Department of State's annual ranking of States engaged in the fight against trafficking.[17] This important report adopts the standards set by the *Human Trafficking Victims Protection Act*[18] as its assessment parameters. As a result of the downgrading from "Tier 1" in 2018 (State that fully complies with these standards), to "Tier 2" in 2019 (State that does not fully comply with these standards), the international reputation of the Italian Government suffered a severe blow. It lost the opportunity to give a concrete signal of Italy's international commitment by lending the new bill a wider scope and a different approach to transnational investigations.

The US Government has recently published the 2021 report.[19] The Italian downgrading to the "Tier 2" position has been confirmed. It can therefore be said, as was to be expected, that there has been no particular recognition of any positive effects of the new Italian law either as regards the international reputation of the Italian State or in terms of the adequacy of domestic measures aimed at more effectively combating the phenomena of migrant smuggling. We will further discuss this latter topic. But it is worth underlining that a Parliament made up of large groups of political forces which proudly declared themselves to be advocates of national sovereignty (*sovraniste*) seemed to have refrained from exercising its powers of control over the Government. Such control could be effected, for example, by setting maximum limits on the duration of operations (which could be extended subject to parliamentary

16 See Laura Salvadego, *The Respect for Fundamental Rights in the Fight against Human Trafficking and Migrant Smuggling across the Central Mediterranean Sea*, Leiden, Boston, 2019.

17 United States Department of State, *Trafficking in persons report*, June 2021, available here: https://www.state.gov/wp-content/uploads/2021/07/TIP_Report_Final_20210701.pdf.

18 Available at www.state.gov/international-and-domestic-law/. US legislation on this topic is being continuously updated and emended. At the time of writing a new bill on the same topic was about to be introduced; it is available at https://www.congress.gov/bill/115th-congress/senate-bill/1312.

19 Available at www.state.gov/wp-content/uploads/2020/06/2020-TIP-Report-Complete-062420-FINAL.pdf.

authorization) and by specifying the equipment to be provided, the minimum rank and level of training of the law enforcement agents involved, whether and if so what type of immunity from civil and criminal cases must be provided to foreign agents, and so on.

Article 4 of the *Decreto sicurezza* has given rise to concern for other reasons as well. It claims that there is a situation of extraordinary need and urgency which would justify the use of a faster procedure for approving laws – something considered "exceptional" under the Italian Constitution[20] – and a derogation from the ordinary legislative procedure. According to the official data issued by the Italian Ministry of the Interior, in the very period in which the decree was converted into law landings of migrants decreased by more than ninety percent.[21] It is not clear, therefore, what extraordinary reasons of need and urgency induced the Government to attribute to the Minister of the Interior even the power to close ports, by decree, for "violations of the immigration laws in force".[22]

3 Conclusion

Italy has undertaken a first effort to make the special investigation techniques adopted compliant with its obligations at a international level. Beyond the legal "labels" and the political proclamations regarding the sensitive topic of managing illegal migrant flows, it is doubtful, however, that it will reach the set targets. From the evidence provided so far, it should be clear that the provisions of the *Decreto Sicurezza* providing for financial support to undercover operations hosting foreign law enforcement agents on Italian territory, and apparently focused on the fight against criminal networks managing irregular migration, may possibly be exploited to a greater extent in the context of investigations into other transnational crimes. For example, in the efforts to prevent and suppress other "serious crimes" like terrorism or illicit drug networks or

20 See art. 77 of the Italian Constitution: "The Government may not, without an enabling act from the Houses, issue a decree having force of law. When the Government, in case of necessity and urgency, adopts under its own responsibility a temporary measure, it shall introduce such measure to Parliament for transposition into law".

21 A daily update on the official data can be found here: www.interno.gov.it/sites/default/files/2020-06/cruscotto_statistico_giornaliero_30-06-2020.pdf.

22 See art. 1, para. 1 of the *Decreto Sicurezza*.

financial criminal offences.[23] But the new provision regarding undercover missions that can take place in Italy is drafted in a very terse manner. In accepting the absence of clearly stated rules, the Parliament has refused to exercise its "sovereign" powers and has contradicted itself by granting the Government, and mainly the Ministry of the Interior, a blank cheque which may lead to unpredictable outcomes.

23 A list of serious crimes that are regulated at EU level can be found in Article 83 (1) TFEU. It includes terrorism and other crimes such as computer crime, organised crime, money laundering, trafficking in human beings and sexual exploitation of women and children, illicit drug trafficking, illicit arms trafficking, corruption and counterfeiting of means of payment. For the relevant instruments of EU Criminal Law see: Council of the European Union, *European Union instruments in the field of criminal law and related texts*, Brussels, December 2019. Among scholars, on the topic: Valsamis Mitsilegas, *EU Criminal Law*, Oxford, Portland, 2009; Valsamis Mitsilegas, Maria Bergström and Theodore Konstadinides, *Research Handbook on EU Criminal Law*, London, 2016.

www.ingramcontent.com/pod-product-compliance
Lightning Source LLC
Chambersburg PA
CBHW071352230926
51846CB00002B/522